JUMBLE Christmas!

'Tis the season for puzzles!

Henri Arnold,
Bob Lee,
David L. Hoyt
and Jeff Knurek

TRIUMPH
BOOKS

For further information, con tact:
Triumph Books LLC
814 North Franklin Street
Chicago, Illinois 60610
Phone: (312) 337-0747
www.triumphbooks.com

Printed in U.S.A.

ISBN: 978-1-63727-182-7

Design by Sue Knopf

Contents

Classic Puzzles
1–25...Page 1

Daily Puzzles
26–160...Page 27

Challenger Puzzles
161–180...Page 163

Answers
Page 184

JUMBLE®

Christmas

Classic Puzzles

JUMBLE®

Unscramble these four Jumbles, one letter to each square, to form four ordinary words.

NEVET

BLAYM

GUEMLE

NIPPOL

I'm getting one

Me, too

WHEN ADDING MACHINES WERE FIRST INTRODUCED THEY WERE SO SUCCESSFUL THAT THEY BEGAN TO DO THIS.

Now arrange the circled letters to form the surprise answer, as suggested by the above cartoon.

Print answer here "  "

JUMBLE®

Unscramble these four Jumbles, one letter
to each square, to form four ordinary words.

CLATH

EAGAD

GICART

VOUDER

SHE SAID HE WAS
HER PET PROJECT
WHICH MUST BE WHY
SHE TRIED TO
DO THIS.

Now arrange the circled letters
to form the surprise answer, as
suggested by the above cartoon.

Print answer here ⬡⬡⬡⬡⬡ HIM LIKE A ⬡⬡⬡

JUMBLE®

Unscramble these four Jumbles, one letter
to each square, to form four ordinary words.

IDDEA

ARZYC

CARNID

TICEXE

WHAT THEY DID
WHEN THAT MAN
FELL OFF THE
HORSE.

Now arrange the circled letters
to form the surprise answer, as
suggested by the above cartoon.

Print answer
here "☐☐ - ☐☐☐☐☐" HIM

JUMBLE®

Unscramble these four Jumbles, one letter to each square, to form four ordinary words.

TOOPH

KLAYB

TELTAC

JELDIA

THEY CALLED THAT ECCENTRIC INVENTOR A CRACKPOT UNTIL HE DID THIS.

Now arrange the circled letters to form the surprise answer, as suggested by the above cartoon.

Print answer here ☐☐☐ THE ☐☐☐☐☐☐☐

JUMBLE®

Unscramble these four Jumbles, one letter
to each square, to form four ordinary words.

POASY

MARFE

YORRAS

ENCOUB

DIRGE

DO ZOMBIES LIKE
BEING DEAD?

Now arrange the circled letters
to form the surprise answer, as
suggested by the above cartoon.

Print answer here " ☐☐ ☐☐☐☐☐☐ "

JUMBLE®

Unscramble these four Jumbles, one letter
to each square, to form four ordinary words.

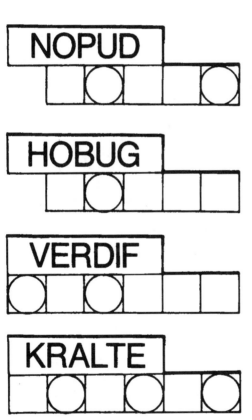

NOPUD

HOBUG

VERDIF

KRALTE

WHAT CAUSED
THE PUNCTURE IN
THE TIRE?

Now arrange the circled letters
to form the surprise answer, as
suggested by the above cartoon.

Print answer here A ⬚⬚⬚⬚⬚ IN THE ⬚⬚⬚⬚

JUMBLE®

Unscramble these four Jumbles, one letter to each square, to form four ordinary words.

SOKYM

DYSIA

TOSFRY

FLUTIP

WHAT ICE IS.

Now arrange the circled letters to form the surprise answer, as suggested by the above cartoon.

Print answer here " ⬜⬜⬜⬜ " ⬜⬜⬜⬜⬜

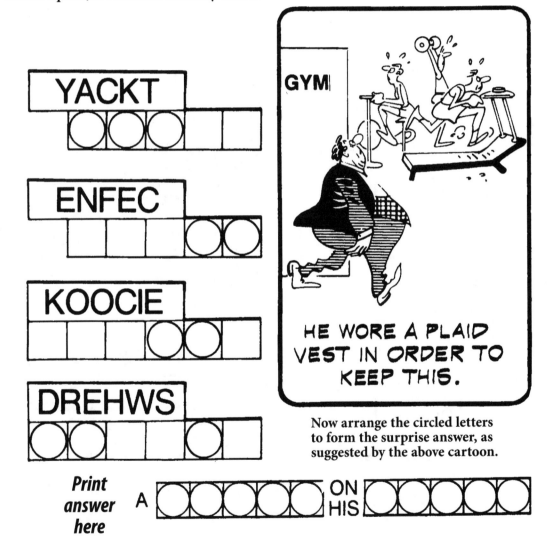

JUMBLE®

Unscramble these four Jumbles, one letter
to each square, to form four ordinary words.

YACKT

ENFEC

KOOCIE

DREHWS

GYM

HE WORE A PLAID
VEST IN ORDER TO
KEEP THIS.

Now arrange the circled letters
to form the surprise answer, as
suggested by the above cartoon.

Print
answer
here

A ☐☐☐☐☐ ON
HIS ☐☐☐☐☐

JUMBLE®

Unscramble these four Jumbles, one letter
to each square, to form four ordinary words.

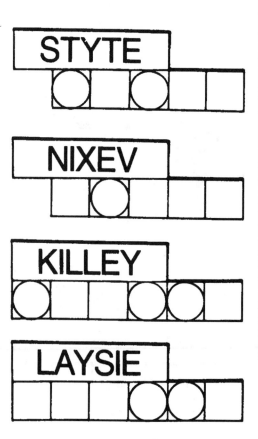

STYTE

NIXEV

KILLEY

LAYSIE

He never told the truth
and he never will

HILL

WHAT LIARS DO
AFTER THEY DIE.

Now arrange the circled letters
to form the surprise answer, as
suggested by the above cartoon.

Print answer here

JUMBLE

Unscramble these four Jumbles, one letter
to each square, to form four ordinary words.

REFIA

KAROC

YERTOP

DULSHO

His work seems to reflect
his line of chatter

YAK YAK
YAK

WOULD YOU BELIEVE
A PAINTER WHO
DID THIS?

Now arrange the circled letters
to form the surprise answer, as
suggested by the above cartoon.

Print
answer
here

IT
ON

JUMBLE®

Unscramble these four Jumbles, one letter to each square, to form four ordinary words.

WRONC

MYPTE

JETNUK

NAWDDE

WHAT THE WOLF WHO WAS GOING TO JOIN THE CARD GAME BROUGHT WITH HIM.

Now arrange the circled letters to form the surprise answer, as suggested by the above cartoon.

Print answer here HIS ◯◯◯ " ◯◯◯◯ "

JUMBLE®

Unscramble these four Jumbles, one letter to each square, to form four ordinary words.

SELOU

RETIG

DIEPIT

RUMMUR

WHAT THE SAD TREE SAID AFTER THE AXMAN DID HIS WORK.

Now arrange the circled letters to form the surprise answer, as suggested by the above cartoon.

Print answer here "☐'☐ ☐☐☐☐☐☐☐"

JUMBLE®

Unscramble these four Jumbles, one letter
to each square, to form four ordinary words.

POSOT

THOLC

AIRLAD

GHURNY

A FABULOUSLY
SUCCESSFUL BAKER
MIGHT BRING THESE
WORDS TO MIND.

Now arrange the circled letters
to form the surprise answer, as
suggested by the above cartoon.

Print answer
here

⬡⬡⬡⬡⬡ IN ⬡⬡⬡⬡⬡

JUMBLE®

Unscramble these four Jumbles, one letter
to each square, to form four ordinary words.

IPSOE

TUISE

HERNUT

GOTHET

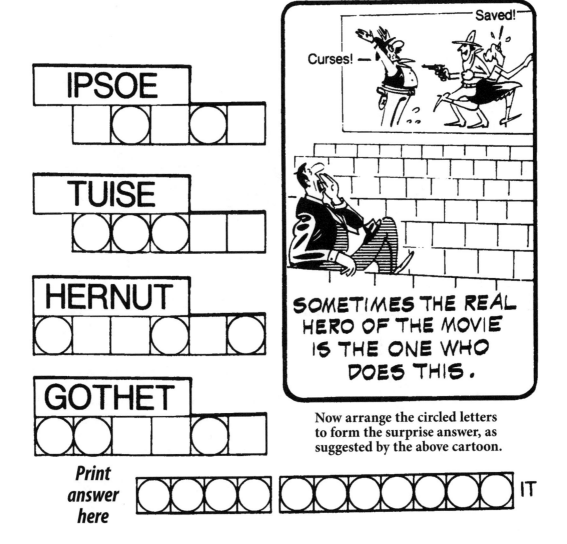

Curses! —   Saved!

SOMETIMES THE REAL
HERO OF THE MOVIE
IS THE ONE WHO
DOES THIS.

Now arrange the circled letters
to form the surprise answer, as
suggested by the above cartoon.

*Print
answer
here*   IT

JUMBLE®

Unscramble these four Jumbles, one letter to each square, to form four ordinary words.

NADDY

LUFOR

INPACT

CLOTUC

WHAT THE GUY WHO CONSTANTLY DRANK HOT CHOCOLATE MUST HAVE BEEN.

Now arrange the circled letters to form the surprise answer, as suggested by the above cartoon.

Print answer here   A "◯◯◯◯◯ ◯◯◯"

JUMBLE®

Unscramble these four Jumbles, one letter
to each square, to form four ordinary words.

TAFUL

ROBIL

LYBBAF

MALEYS

WHEN IS A BOAT
THE CHEAPEST?

Now arrange the circled letters
to form the surprise answer, as
suggested by the above cartoon.

*Print answer
here*   WHEN "◯◯◯◯" ◯◯◯◯
        IT'S A

17

JUMBLE®

Unscramble these four Jumbles, one letter
to each square, to form four ordinary words.

LIDUF

ESHOU

POOPSE

SLAQUL

WHAT THE FEMALE
DINOSAUR SAID TO
HER GROUCHY MATE.

Now arrange the circled letters
to form the surprise answer, as
suggested by the above cartoon.

Print answer here YOU

JUMBLE®

Unscramble these four Jumbles, one letter to each square, to form four ordinary words.

NEWIT

VINEA

LEETEY

ISSUME

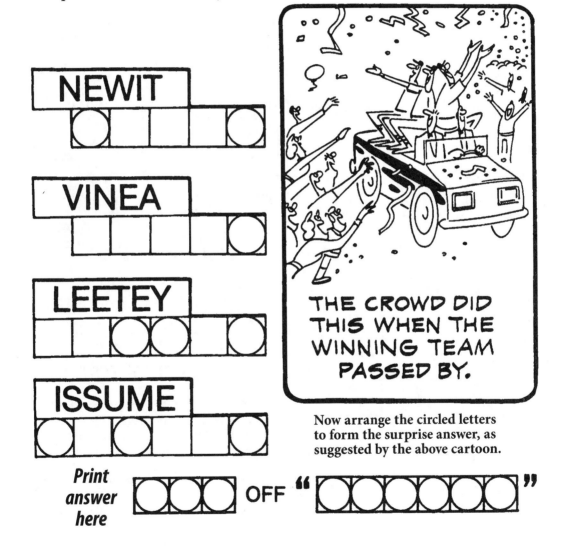

THE CROWD DID THIS WHEN THE WINNING TEAM PASSED BY.

Now arrange the circled letters to form the surprise answer, as suggested by the above cartoon.

Print answer here ☐☐☐ OFF " ☐☐☐☐☐☐ "

JUMBLE

Unscramble these four Jumbles, one letter
to each square, to form four ordinary words.

RUSIV

NILAF

SHAMON

DIASUN

But where will the money come from?

I think I've got an idea

WHAT THE CITY
REQUIRED IN ORDER
TO CLEAN UP THE
AFTERMATH OF A
BIG SNOWSTORM.

Now arrange the circled letters
to form the surprise answer, as
suggested by the above cartoon.

*Print answer
here* A " ⬡⬡⬡⬡⬡ " ⬡⬡⬡⬡

JUMBLE®

Unscramble these four Jumbles, one letter
to each square, to form four ordinary words.

MIDUH

PRIPE

YETTIN

FLEMSY

Villa Ristorante

FAT IS THE
PENALTY FOR
EXCEEDING THIS.

Now arrange the circled letters
to form the surprise answer, as
suggested by the above cartoon.

Print answer here THE ⬡⬡⬡⬡⬡ ⬡⬡⬡⬡⬡

JUMBLE®

Unscramble these four Jumbles, one letter to each square, to form four ordinary words.

EKRIP

TAULD

EUMMUS

REVUPY

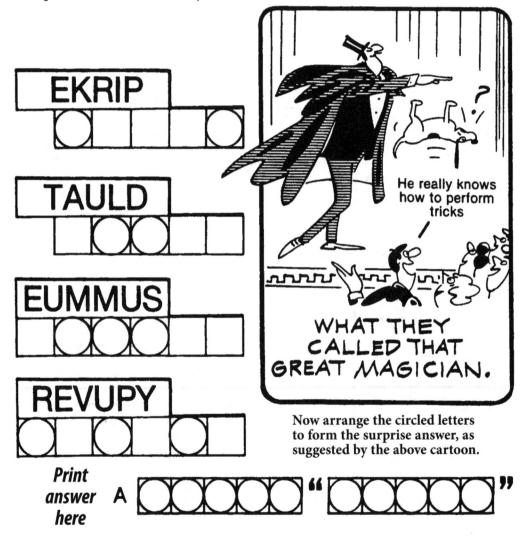

He really knows how to perform tricks

WHAT THEY CALLED THAT GREAT MAGICIAN.

Now arrange the circled letters to form the surprise answer, as suggested by the above cartoon.

Print answer here

A ⬡⬡⬡⬡⬡ " ⬡⬡⬡⬡⬡ "

JUMBLE®

Unscramble these four Jumbles, one letter
to each square, to form four ordinary words.

CHARP

SMACH

ZARABA

LIMUHE

ANOTHER NAME
FOR RABBIT FUR.

Now arrange the circled letters
to form the surprise answer, as
suggested by the above cartoon.

Print answer here ⭕⭕⭕⭕ ⭕⭕⭕

JUMBLE®

Unscramble these four Jumbles, one letter to each square, to form four ordinary words.

YUHRR

KORPE

NAUGIA

BLUTSY

WHAT THE LAME-
BRAIN SAID WHEN
HIS LAWYER TOLD
HIM HE HAD
LOST HIS SUIT.

Now arrange the circled letters to form the surprise answer, as suggested by the above cartoon.

Print
answer
here

I'LL

JUMBLE®

Unscramble these four Jumbles, one letter
to each square, to form four ordinary words.

THISO

RAPAT

SAMTIG

PROTTE

WHAT MANY A
NIGHT SPOT IS.

Now arrange the circled letters
to form the surprise answer, as
suggested by the above cartoon.

Print answer
here A " ◯◯◯◯◯ " ◯◯◯◯

JUMBLE®

Unscramble these four Jumbles, one letter
to each square, to form four ordinary words.

PROAV

BLACE

DAHNED

NUCFED

TOP SECRET

HONK!

THE SECRET AGENT
WAS ALWAYS BLOWING
HIS NOSE BECAUSE
HE HAD THIS.

Now arrange the circled letters
to form the surprise answer, as
suggested by the above cartoon.

Print answer
here   A "⬡⬡⬡⬡⬡" IN THE ⬡⬡⬡⬡

JUMBLE®

Christmas

Daily Puzzles

JUMBLE®

Unscramble these four Jumbles, one letter
to each square, to form four ordinary words.

ROWNC

ILEEX

DAJEGG

TOXREV

THEY WENT TO THAT
ISLAND FOR "TEA"
BECAUSE IT WAS
IN THE MIDDLE
OF THIS.

Now arrange the circled letters
to form the surprise answer, as
suggested by the above cartoon.

Print answer here " ☐☐ - ☐ - ☐☐ "

JUMBLE®

Unscramble these four Jumbles, one letter
to each square, to form four ordinary words.

INTEF

ELCEX

TAIREW

MASHAT

WHAT THE SIGN ON
THE SALES LOT FOR
MOBILE HOMES SAID.

Now arrange the circled letters
to form the surprise answer, as
suggested by the above cartoon.

Print
answer
here

" ⃝⃝⃝⃝⃝⃝ " ⃝⃝⃝⃝⃝⃝⃝

JUMBLE®

Unscramble these four Jumbles, one letter
to each square, to form four ordinary words.

HELIT

LOCCI

PECILS

SARATY

WHAT KIND OF
ANIMAL HELPS
CHASE OUTLAWS?

Now arrange the circled letters
to form the surprise answer, as
suggested by the above cartoon.

Print answer here A "⬡⬡⬡⬡⬡" ⬡⬡⬡

JUMBLE®

Unscramble these four Jumbles, one letter
to each square, to form four ordinary words.

TORIB

ELLAP

ROTRAM

ORTRER

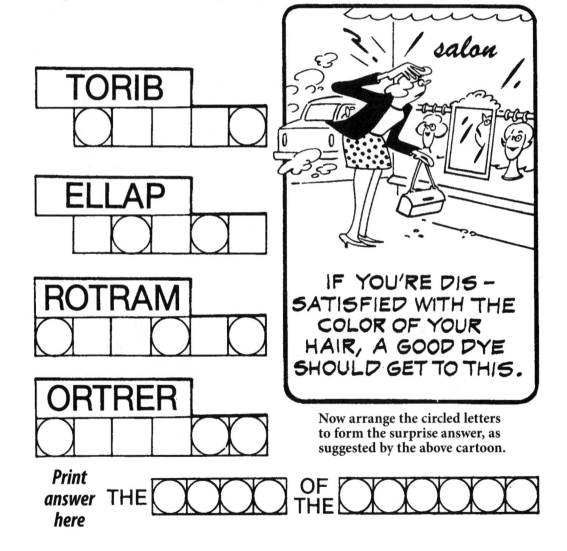

IF YOU'RE DIS-
SATISFIED WITH THE
COLOR OF YOUR
HAIR, A GOOD DYE
SHOULD GET TO THIS.

Now arrange the circled letters
to form the surprise answer, as
suggested by the above cartoon.

*Print
answer
here*
THE ⬡⬡⬡⬡ OF THE ⬡⬡⬡⬡⬡⬡

JUMBLE®

Unscramble these four Jumbles, one letter to each square, to form four ordinary words.

ABOOT

LEVAT

UNGOLE

TRYFOS

Now arrange the circled letters to form the surprise answer, as suggested by the above cartoon.

Print answer here

JUMBLE®

Unscramble these four Jumbles, one letter to each square, to form four ordinary words.

RAYAR

VACHO

LEDENE

COYJEK

WHY IT'S SO
EASY TO MILK
A COW.

Now arrange the circled letters to form the surprise answer, as suggested by the above cartoon.

Print answer here ANY " ☐☐☐☐☐ " ☐☐☐ ☐☐ IT

JUMBLE®

Unscramble these four Jumbles, one letter to each square, to form four ordinary words.

DAMMA

TOAQU

SLOMBY

CREEFI

I find some hidden weakness in his work

WHAT THE POTTER WAS NOTED FOR.

Now arrange the circled letters to form the surprise answer, as suggested by the above cartoon.

Print answer here

HIS " ⬡⬡⬡⬡⬡ " OF ⬡⬡⬡⬡

JUMBLE®

Unscramble these four Jumbles, one letter
to each square, to form four ordinary words.

YACED

UNREP

GLANJE

THAGAS

WHY EVERYONE
LOVES A BANANA.

Now arrange the circled letters
to form the surprise answer, as
suggested by the above cartoon.

Print answer here   IT
HAS   " ☐ ☐☐☐☐ "

JUMBLE®

Unscramble these four Jumbles, one letter to each square, to form four ordinary words.

DEALL

RABIR

THAYCC

GRUIDT

YOU WOULDN'T WANT THIS IN A CEMETERY.

Now arrange the circled letters to form the surprise answer, as suggested by the above cartoon.

Print answer here

TO
BE

JUMBLE®

Unscramble these four Jumbles, one letter
to each square, to form four ordinary words.

LAVIT

ATHEW

LOSFIS

DRENER

Gotta do
some
advertising

Here, you
take these

WHAT AN AIRLINE
MIGHT DO IN ORDER
TO DRUM UP
BUSINESS.

Now arrange the circled letters
to form the surprise answer, as
suggested by the above cartoon.

Print
answer
here

⬡⬡⬡⬡ OUT "⬡⬡⬡⬡⬡⬡"

JUMBLE®

Unscramble these four Jumbles, one letter
to each square, to form four ordinary words.

LONBE

IDLAY

ZEFIRE

NAPTIC

WHAT HAPPENS WHEN
TWO EGOTISTS HAVE
A FALLING OUT.

Now arrange the circled letters
to form the surprise answer, as
suggested by the above cartoon.

Print answer here   IT'S ☐☐ "☐" ☐☐☐ AN "☐"

JUMBLE®

Unscramble these four Jumbles, one letter to each square, to form four ordinary words.

SUMEO

LAVIA

YOGAVE

SAUNAE

My husband will be so proud of me

BARGAIN SALE

SHE'S DETERMINED TO DO THIS, NO MATTER HOW MUCH IT COSTS.

Now arrange the circled letters to form the surprise answer, as suggested by the above cartoon.

Print answer here

JUMBLE®

Unscramble these four Jumbles, one letter
to each square, to form four ordinary words.

YURLS

NEESU

CLAGEY

HISRAP

Let's destroy 'em!

MGR

WHAT DID THEY CALL
THE TEAM MADE UP
OF FRANKENSTEIN
MONSTERS?

Now arrange the circled letters
to form the surprise answer, as
suggested by the above cartoon.

Print answer here THE " ☐☐☐ – ☐☐☐☐☐ "

JUMBLE®

Unscramble these four Jumbles, one letter
to each square, to form four ordinary words.

SASEY

RUZEA

HYCTOU

GERELD

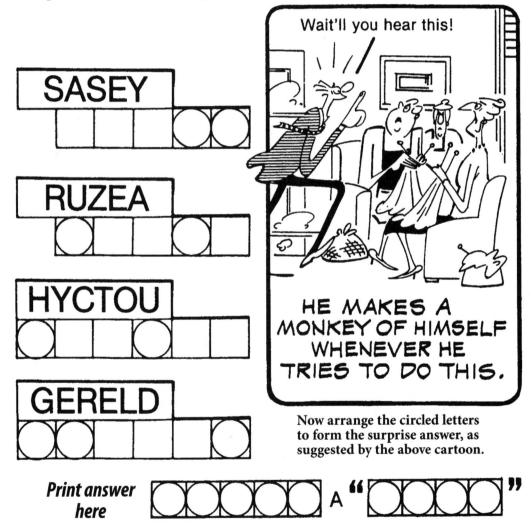

Wait'll you hear this!

HE MAKES A
MONKEY OF HIMSELF
WHENEVER HE
TRIES TO DO THIS.

Now arrange the circled letters
to form the surprise answer, as
suggested by the above cartoon.

Print answer here ◯◯◯◯◯ A "◯◯◯◯"

JUMBLE®

Unscramble these four Jumbles, one letter
to each square, to form four ordinary words.

TEMPY

RAAMO

CLIPEN

MESORK

WHY THE WORMS
DIDN'T ENTER NOAH'S
ARK IN "PAIRS."

Now arrange the circled letters
to form the surprise answer, as
suggested by the above cartoon.

*Print
answer
here* THEY ☐☐☐☐☐ IN ☐☐☐☐☐☐☐

JUMBLE®

Unscramble these four Jumbles, one letter
to each square, to form four ordinary words.

LIBOR

NINOO

SWAALY

TOYBUN

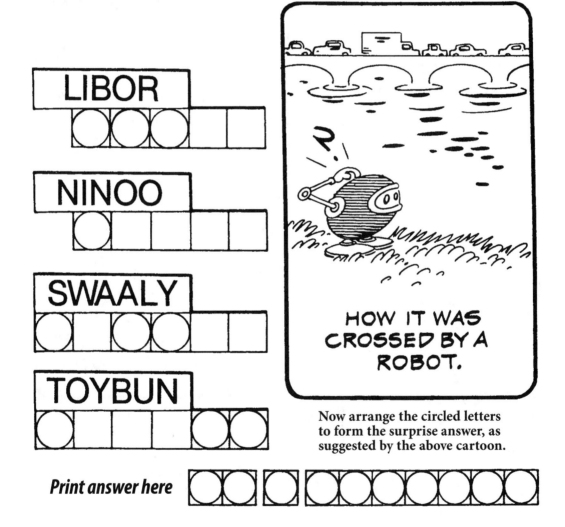

HOW IT WAS
CROSSED BY A
ROBOT.

Now arrange the circled letters
to form the surprise answer, as
suggested by the above cartoon.

Print answer here

JUMBLE®

Unscramble these four Jumbles, one letter
to each square, to form four ordinary words.

MORIN

TRIGE

SHRAIG

PETICK

WHAT SHE SAID
ABOUT THEIR NEW
HOUSE THAT LOOKED
LIKE A MATCHBOX.

Now arrange the circled letters
to form the surprise answer, as
suggested by the above cartoon.

Print answer here   IT'S " ◯◯◯◯◯◯◯◯◯ "

JUMBLE®

Unscramble these four Jumbles, one letter to each square, to form four ordinary words.

GYNAT

WHYSO

QUILOR

LETTAC

Tsk tsk—but don't let it happen again

WHAT HAPPENED WHEN THE LEFT HALF OF THE CAKE DISAPPEARED?

Now arrange the circled letters to form the surprise answer, as suggested by the above cartoon.

Print answer here IT WAS " ☐☐☐ ☐☐☐☐☐ "

JUMBLE®

Unscramble these four Jumbles, one letter
to each square, to form four ordinary words.

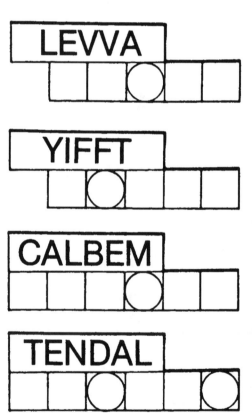

LEVVA

YIFFT

CALBEM

TENDAL

WHEN HE LOST HIS
KEYS AND COULDN'T
GET IN, HE RAN A-
ROUND THE HOUSE
UNTIL HE WAS THIS.

Now arrange the circled letters
to form the surprise answer, as
suggested by the above cartoon.

Print answer here

JUMBLE®

Unscramble these four Jumbles, one letter
to each square, to form four ordinary words.

MYNAL

LAHZE

PORRAL

SPYNAP

MAIL

WHAT THAT
POPULAR CHEF
CORRESPONDS WITH.

Now arrange the circled letters
to form the surprise answer, as
suggested by the above cartoon.

**Print answer
here** ◯◯◯ "◯◯◯" ◯◯◯◯

JUMBLE®

Unscramble these four Jumbles, one letter
to each square, to form four ordinary words.

OXPRY

FEYHT

DABALL

SUNGUF

WHAT SHE SAID
WHEN HER REJECTED
SUITOR THREATENED
TO JUMP OFF
THE CLIFF.

Now arrange the circled letters
to form the surprise answer, as
suggested by the above cartoon.

*Print
answer
here*   THAT'S ☐☐☐☐ A " ☐☐☐☐☐ "

JUMBLE®

Unscramble these four Jumbles, one letter to each square, to form four ordinary words.

YINCC

NAIGG

SHEERA

CHINTS

HE HAD NO PROBLEM KEEPING UP HIS END OF THE CONVERSATION, BUT A LOT OF TROUBLE DOING THIS.

Now arrange the circled letters to form the surprise answer, as suggested by the above cartoon.

Print answer here

JUMBLE®

Unscramble these four Jumbles, one letter
to each square, to form four ordinary words.

LATUF

GUBOH

CAFFEE

THOGTE

YOU'LL NEVER LOSE
WEIGHT IF YOU TRY
TO DO NO MORE
THAN THIS.

Now arrange the circled letters
to form the surprise answer, as
suggested by the above cartoon.

Print answer here ◯◯◯◯◯ IT ◯◯◯

JUMBLE®

Unscramble these four Jumbles, one letter
to each square, to form four ordinary words.

KOESM

GRABE

YATAPH

INFFUM

WHAT THE
FRUSTRATED ACTOR
TURNED BUTCHER
KNEW HOW TO DO.

Now arrange the circled letters
to form the surprise answer, as
suggested by the above cartoon.

Print answer here

JUMBLE®

Unscramble these four Jumbles, one letter
to each square, to form four ordinary words.

CANKK

WOSOP

KLACEY

HUCCOR

WHAT KIND OF MUSIC
DO YOU GET WHEN
YOU THROW A STONE
INTO THE WATER?

Now arrange the circled letters
to form the surprise answer, as
suggested by the above cartoon.

Print answer here " ⬡⬡⬡⬡⬡⬡ " ⬡⬡⬡⬡

JUMBLE ®

Unscramble these four Jumbles, one letter
to each square, to form four ordinary words.

GGION

BYOLB

ECATHD

STAGEK

It's so crowded in there.

These are great!

They're splinter-proof.

AFTER THE DUTCH STARTED
MAKING WOODEN SHOES,
STORES WERE ---

Now arrange the circled letters
to form the surprise answer, as
suggested by the above cartoon.

Print answer here

53

JUMBLE®

Unscramble these four Jumbles, one letter
to each square, to form four ordinary words.

NOYHE

LEDYI

PURYMG

EESAWL

No more stalling.
How come?
We said so.
How come?
You need your sleep.
How come?

THE BOY WHO QUESTIONED
EVERY REQUEST FROM HIS
PARENTS WAS A ---

Now arrange the circled letters
to form the surprise answer, as
suggested by the above cartoon.

Print answer here "  "

JUMBLE®

Unscramble these four Jumbles, one letter to each square, to form four ordinary words.

FEHTT

OKVEE

NARYCN

MIWYSH

What are you doing? Get upstairs and take a bath, young man!

Can I take one in the morning?

THE CHILD GOT MUDDY PLAYING OUTSIDE AND WOULD END UP ---

Now arrange the circled letters to form the surprise answer, as suggested by the above cartoon.

Print answer here

JUMBLE®

Unscramble these four Jumbles, one letter
to each square, to form four ordinary words.

TISUE

DOYDL

LMHAYN

LEYILK

We shall face off on the
11th at noon at Weehawken
Park. Do you accept?

I accept.

WHEN BURR CHALLENGED
HAMILTON TO A BATTLE
USING PISTOLS, IT WAS ---

Now arrange the circled letters
to form the surprise answer, as
suggested by the above cartoon.

Print
answer
here

"⬡⬡⬡⬡-⬡" ⬡⬡⬡⬡⬡

JUMBLE®

Unscramble these four Jumbles, one letter to each square, to form four ordinary words.

DEROO

LUEED

OMLEVU

SARHHT

Yes. I know. Enough already.

These are the best boots ever! I can't believe how comfortable they are. Wow!

SLEEPY HOLLOW'S LEGEND-ARY HORSEMAN LOVED HIS NEW BOOTS AND WAS ---

Now arrange the circled letters to form the surprise answer, as suggested by the above cartoon.

Print answer here

JUMBLE®

Unscramble these four Jumbles, one letter
to each square, to form four ordinary words.

ZIOGM

SIHKW

NWENIR

UGATOE

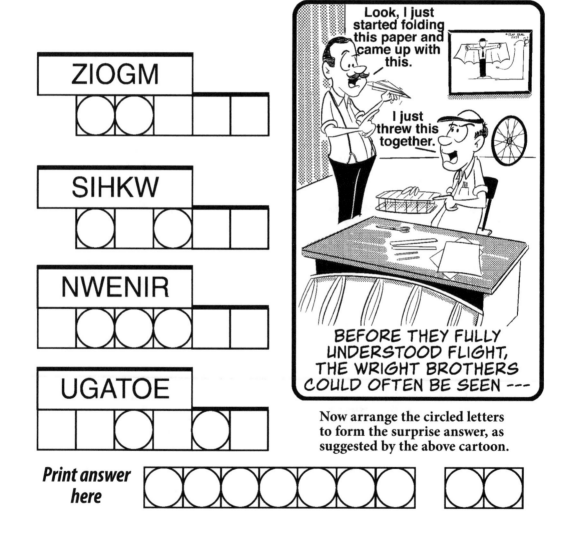

Look, I just
started folding
this paper and
came up with
this.

I just
threw this
together.

BEFORE THEY FULLY
UNDERSTOOD FLIGHT,
THE WRIGHT BROTHERS
COULD OFTEN BE SEEN ---

Now arrange the circled letters
to form the surprise answer, as
suggested by the above cartoon.

**Print answer
here**

JUMBLE®

Unscramble these four Jumbles, one letter
to each square, to form four ordinary words.

DAEIB
○○ ○

UNCOE
□□ ○○

DURRED
○ ○ ○

SPYAMW
□ ○ ○

Will this
work?

Whoa!
I just
needed
it for a
T-shirt.

AFTER ASKING THE JUMBLE
ARTIST TO HELP HER GET ON
"THE PRICE IS RIGHT," HE ---

Now arrange the circled letters
to form the surprise answer, as
suggested by the above cartoon.

**Print answer
here** ○○○○ ○○○○○

JUMBLE®

Unscramble these four Jumbles, one letter
to each square, to form four ordinary words.

TWESP

FAREW

SLUBEH

EECDTT

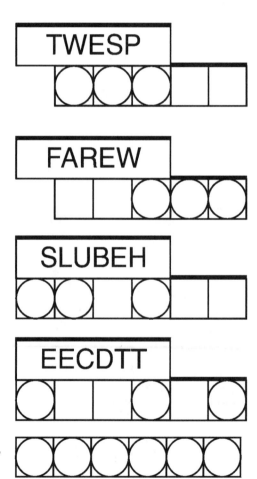

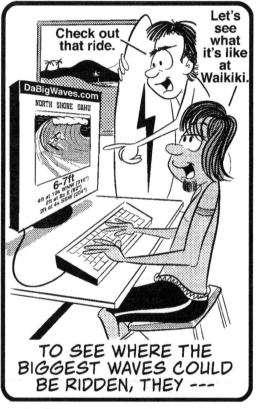

Check out that ride.

Let's see what it's like at Waikiki.

DaBigWaves.com
NORTH SHORE OAHU
6-7ft
4ft at 10s WNW (310°)
2ft at 8s E (82°)
2ft at 4s SSW (204°)

TO SEE WHERE THE
BIGGEST WAVES COULD
BE RIDDEN, THEY ---

Now arrange the circled letters
to form the surprise answer, as
suggested by the above cartoon.

Print answer here

JUMBLE®

Unscramble these four Jumbles, one letter
to each square, to form four ordinary words.

MUPEL

LYLTA

RUGIEF

COADRC

What century is this from?

I guess it's time to say goodbye.

BICYCLE Spoken Here

HER OLD 10-SPEED
WAS WAY BEYOND
REPAIR AND WAS AT
THE END OF ITS ---

Now arrange the circled letters
to form the surprise answer, as
suggested by the above cartoon.

Print answer here

JUMBLE®

Unscramble these four Jumbles, one letter
to each square, to form four ordinary words.

DYIDG

LIPUT

CETEID

SABBRO

Ouch! Did you leave all the sea urchins around?

It wasn't me! It was him!

Oh sure, blame me!

HE BLAMED ANOTHER
SEA LION, BUT THE SEA
LION SAID IT WAS THE ---

Now arrange the circled letters
to form the surprise answer, as
suggested by the above cartoon.

Print answer here " ⬡⬡⬡⬡⬡ " ⬡⬡⬡

JUMBLE®

Unscramble these four Jumbles, one letter
to each square, to form four ordinary words.

TUYHO

SBNIO

KARYEB

TUTWIO

Go inside until
you can be nice
to your sister!

What?
She asked
me to tie
her shoes,
so I tied
them.

He
did
it!

WHEN HER BROTHER TIED
HER SHOES TOGETHER,
HE WAS BEING A ---

Now arrange the circled letters
to form the surprise answer, as
suggested by the above cartoon.

Print answer "⬡⬡⬡⬡⬡⬡" ⬡⬡⬡
here

JUMBLE®

Unscramble these four Jumbles, one letter to each square, to form four ordinary words.

ESIGN

GYBUR

GLEEPD

RONELG

WHEN THEY FOUND A BAG OF PEANUTS AT THE GRAND CANYON, THE SQUIRRELS ---

Now arrange the circled letters to form the surprise answer, as suggested by the above cartoon.

Print answer here

JUMBLE®

Unscramble these four Jumbles, one letter
to each square, to form four ordinary words.

YOVEN

SSULH

IVENDI

DNEWTA

I'll just
have my
eggs the
usual way.
And coffee,
black.

You
need
to turn
that
frown
around.

THE CUSTOMER WAS A
PESSIMIST AND ORDERED
HIS EGGS ---

Now arrange the circled letters
to form the surprise answer, as
suggested by the above cartoon.

**Print
answer
here**

◯◯◯◯◯ - ◯◯◯◯ ◯◯◯◯

JUMBLE®

Unscramble these four Jumbles, one letter to each square, to form four ordinary words.

DAGUR

SEEAC

DOTUIS

PRISTC

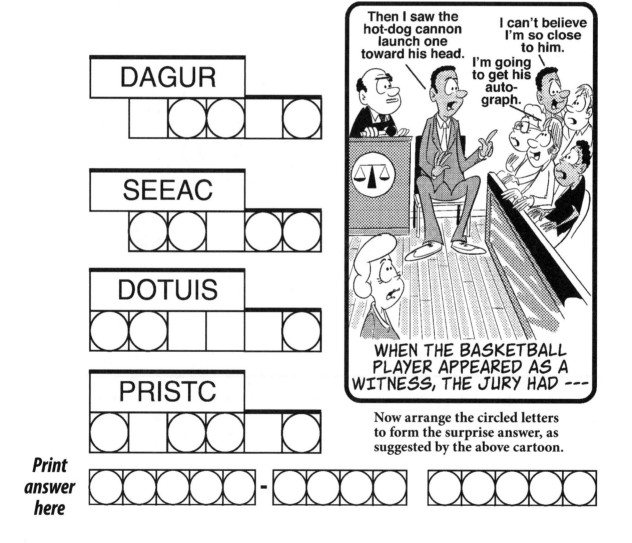

Then I saw the hot-dog cannon launch one toward his head.

I can't believe I'm so close to him.

I'm going to get his auto-graph.

WHEN THE BASKETBALL PLAYER APPEARED AS A WITNESS, THE JURY HAD ---

Now arrange the circled letters to form the surprise answer, as suggested by the above cartoon.

Print answer here

◯◯◯◯◯ - ◯◯◯◯ ◯◯◯◯◯

JUMBLE®

Unscramble these four Jumbles, one letter
to each square, to form four ordinary words.

SEQUT

HYRIA

NAGEAD

PRYUSY

So, we agree on this design?

I'll let the mint know.

Yes. Let's run with that.

THE MINT WHERE THE
WASHINGTON 25-CENT
COINS WERE PRODUCED
WAS THE ---

Now arrange the circled letters
to form the surprise answer, as
suggested by the above cartoon.

Print
answer
here

JUMBLE®

Unscramble these four Jumbles, one letter to each square, to form four ordinary words.

AZGUE

CLEET

DASIRU

RAYPAL

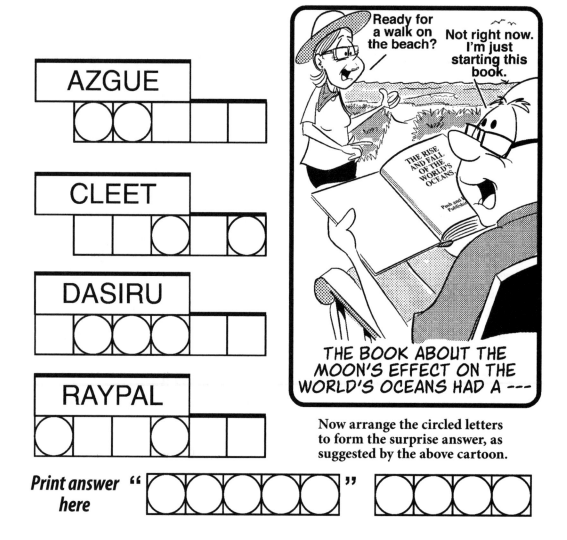

Ready for a walk on the beach?

Not right now. I'm just starting this book.

THE RISE AND FALL OF THE WORLD'S OCEANS

THE BOOK ABOUT THE MOON'S EFFECT ON THE WORLD'S OCEANS HAD A ---

Now arrange the circled letters to form the surprise answer, as suggested by the above cartoon.

Print answer here " ⚪⚪⚪⚪⚪ " ⚪⚪⚪⚪

JUMBLE®

Unscramble these four Jumbles, one letter
to each square, to form four ordinary words.

ZNOOE

UYPPP

SGIDET

SCUURK

It looks fast!

It is! We put a turbo in it.

HAPPY SPOON

THE CHEF WHO WAS A
PART-TIME RACE CAR
DRIVER DROVE A CAR
THAT WAS ---

Now arrange the circled letters
to form the surprise answer, as
suggested by the above cartoon.

Print answer here

JUMBLE®

Unscramble these four Jumbles, one letter to each square, to form four ordinary words.

RHUSE

INTAG

TUWALO

TYSPAR

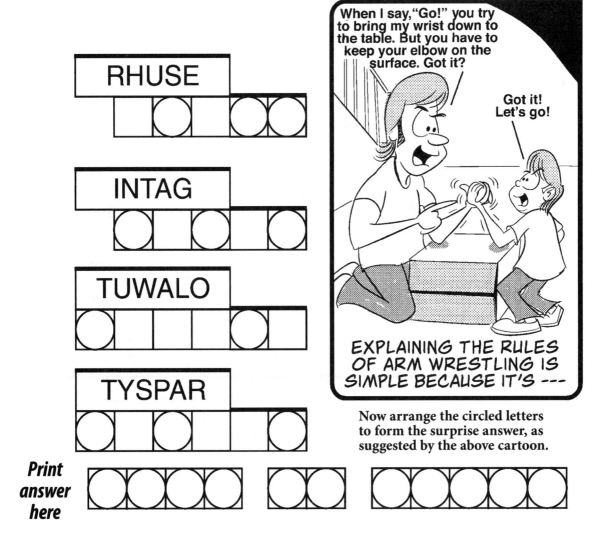

When I say, "Go!" you try to bring my wrist down to the table. But you have to keep your elbow on the surface. Got it?

Got it! Let's go!

EXPLAINING THE RULES OF ARM WRESTLING IS SIMPLE BECAUSE IT'S ---

Now arrange the circled letters to form the surprise answer, as suggested by the above cartoon.

Print answer here

JUMBLE®

Unscramble these four Jumbles, one letter
to each square, to form four ordinary words.

ZAUZB

PRYEK

WERHDS

DAYALM

Let your readers know
that we will be welcoming
them on October 31.

HE ANNOUNCED WHEN
MOUNT RUSHMORE
WOULD BE COMPLETED
TO GIVE PEOPLE A ---

Now arrange the circled letters
to form the surprise answer, as
suggested by the above cartoon.

Print answer here

JUMBLE®

Unscramble these four Jumbles, one letter to each square, to form four ordinary words.

VIYRP

RRNUE

FITANN

TOHNPO

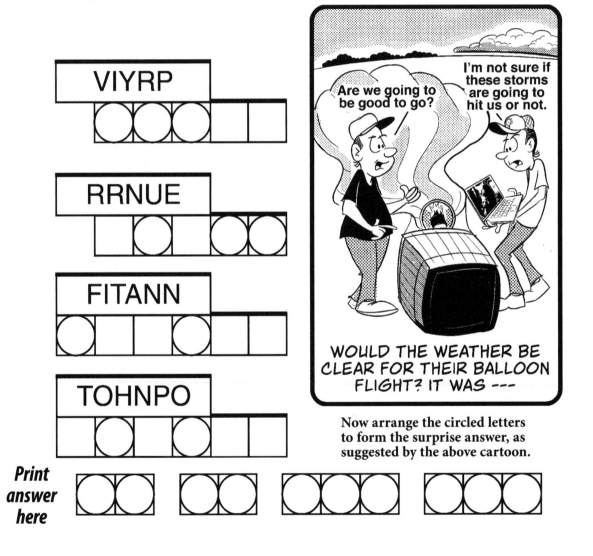

Are we going to be good to go?

I'm not sure if these storms are going to hit us or not.

WOULD THE WEATHER BE CLEAR FOR THEIR BALLOON FLIGHT? IT WAS ---

Now arrange the circled letters to form the surprise answer, as suggested by the above cartoon.

Print answer here

JUMBLE®

Unscramble these four Jumbles, one letter to each square, to form four ordinary words.

IGTDI

TOODU

NAGELC

TRFOOG

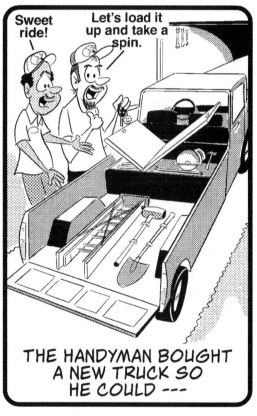

Sweet ride!

Let's load it up and take a spin.

THE HANDYMAN BOUGHT A NEW TRUCK SO HE COULD ---

Now arrange the circled letters to form the surprise answer, as suggested by the above cartoon.

Print answer here

JUMBLE®

Unscramble these four Jumbles, one letter to each square, to form four ordinary words.

SAIDY

UTTAN

ABRREB

DULPED

Nobody has overseen more cases than him.

You may be seated.

Nobody is more fair than him.

CONSIDERED TO BE EXCEPTIONALLY HONEST, THE JUDGE WAS --

Now arrange the circled letters to form the surprise answer, as suggested by the above cartoon.

Print answer here

JUMBLE

Unscramble these four Jumbles, one letter
to each square, to form four ordinary words.

NASTL

RUFTI

MOABOB

TELVEV

These are worth every penny! I can't even see these without a microscope.

Look at this one in the eye of the needle.

AFTER SPECIALIZING IN
MINIATURE SCULPTURES,
WILLARD WIGAN MADE A ---

Now arrange the circled letters
to form the surprise answer, as
suggested by the above cartoon.

Print
answer
here

75

JUMBLE®

Unscramble these four Jumbles, one letter to each square, to form four ordinary words.

LAPTN

BIHTA

LWWIOL

FAYTIR

FINISH

Look at him go!

No one is even close to him.

THE MARATHON'S FINISH WASN'T EVEN CLOSE. THE WINNER ---

Now arrange the circled letters to form the surprise answer, as suggested by the above cartoon.

Print answer here

JUMBLE®

Unscramble these four Jumbles, one letter to each square, to form four ordinary words.

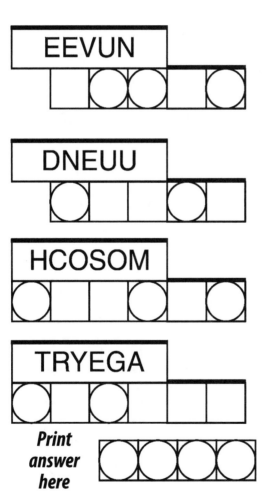

EEVUN

DNEUU

HCOSOM

TRYEGA

Did you get all the snacks we need?

Yep!

Looks like you got everything on the list.

WHEN ASKED IF HE'D BOUGHT AMPLE SUPPLIES FOR THE PARTY, HE SAID ---

Now arrange the circled letters to form the surprise answer, as suggested by the above cartoon.

Print answer here

JUMBLE®

Unscramble these four Jumbles, one letter
to each square, to form four ordinary words.

DREEL
◯◯◯◯◯

SMAEH
◯◯◯◯◯

BCUILP
◯◯◯◯◯◯

GUETAO
◯◯◯◯◯◯

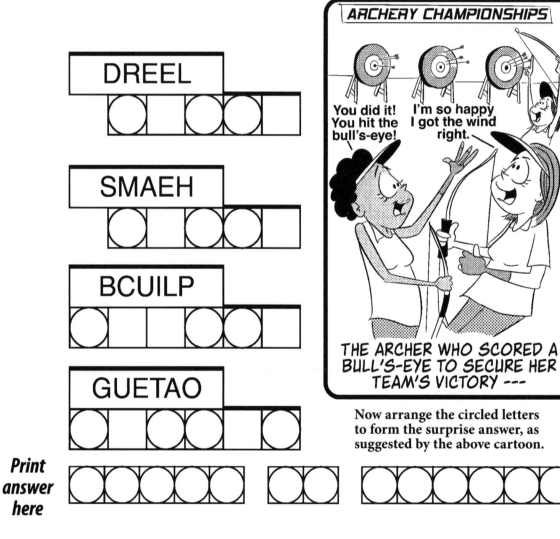

ARCHERY CHAMPIONSHIPS

You did it!
You hit the
bull's-eye!

I'm so happy
I got the wind
right.

THE ARCHER WHO SCORED A
BULL'S-EYE TO SECURE HER
TEAM'S VICTORY ---

Now arrange the circled letters
to form the surprise answer, as
suggested by the above cartoon.

*Print
answer
here*

◯◯◯◯◯   ◯◯   ◯◯◯◯◯◯◯

JUMBLE®

Unscramble these four Jumbles, one letter to each square, to form four ordinary words.

NOTIX

VFREE

POYOKS

SADLIN

Smile!

Hold your ball higher.

Let's get everyone in there.

AFTER BOWLING A 300 GAME, PEOPLE WANTED THE BOWLER TO---

Now arrange the circled letters to form the surprise answer, as suggested by the above cartoon.

Print answer here

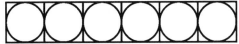 

JUMBLE ®

Unscramble these four Jumbles, one letter to each square, to form four ordinary words.

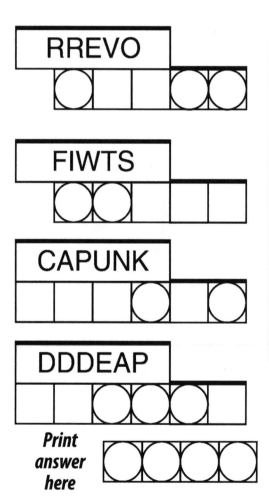

RREVO

FIWTS

CAPUNK

DDDEAP

WHEN THE JUMBLE ARTIST SKETCHED HIS WORK AREA, IT INCLUDED A ---

Now arrange the circled letters to form the surprise answer, as suggested by the above cartoon.

Print answer here

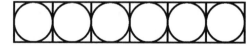

JUMBLE®

Unscramble these four Jumbles, one letter to each square, to form four ordinary words.

IGIRD

RHHAS

EOSLON

TOSYTP

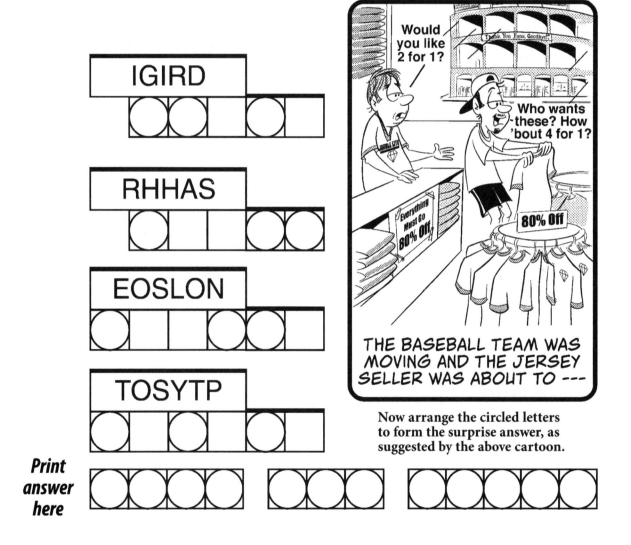

Would you like 2 for 1?

Thank You Fans, Goodbye!

Who wants these? How 'bout 4 for 1?

Everything Must Go 80% Off

80% Off

THE BASEBALL TEAM WAS MOVING AND THE JERSEY SELLER WAS ABOUT TO ---

Now arrange the circled letters to form the surprise answer, as suggested by the above cartoon.

Print answer here

JUMBLE®

Unscramble these four Jumbles, one letter to each square, to form four ordinary words.

VUMEA

OBTOA

SINBHA

CADILP

WHEN THE PIRATE WITH THE PEG LEG WAS TOLD TO WALK THE PLANK, HE WAS---

Now arrange the circled letters to form the surprise answer, as suggested by the above cartoon.

Print answer here

JUMBLE®

Unscramble these four Jumbles, one letter
to each square, to form four ordinary words.

VERPO

THAWC

NWORTH

OLAFTA

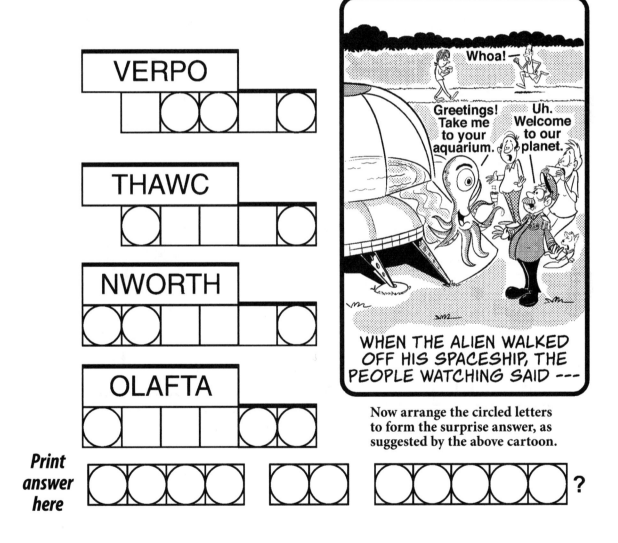

Whoa!

Greetings!
Take me
to your
aquarium.

Uh.
Welcome
to our
planet.

WHEN THE ALIEN WALKED
OFF HIS SPACESHIP, THE
PEOPLE WATCHING SAID ---

Now arrange the circled letters
to form the surprise answer, as
suggested by the above cartoon.

*Print
answer
here*

?

JUMBLE®

Unscramble these four Jumbles, one letter to each square, to form four ordinary words.

PKIMS

EELVA

ETTINN

TGREFO

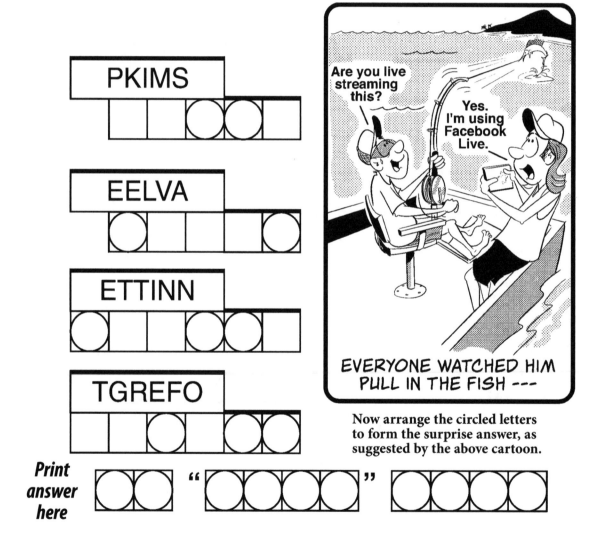

Are you live streaming this?

Yes. I'm using Facebook Live.

EVERYONE WATCHED HIM PULL IN THE FISH ---

Now arrange the circled letters to form the surprise answer, as suggested by the above cartoon.

Print answer here

[ ] "[ ]" [ ]

JUMBLE®

Unscramble these four Jumbles, one letter
to each square, to form four ordinary words.

HIWEG

DENUC

LORENL

CUBNOE

Got it!

These
workers are
some of the
best.

They
work
well
together.

IT TOOK MANY WORKERS
TO MAN THE OFFSHORE
RIG. TOGETHER, THEY
DRILLED FOR ---

Now arrange the circled letters
to form the surprise answer, as
suggested by the above cartoon.

Print answer "⬜⬜⬜⬜⬜⬜" ⬜⬜⬜
here

JUMBLE®

Unscramble these four Jumbles, one letter
to each square, to form four ordinary words.

GILOC
◯◯◯ ◯◯

NODUW
◯◯◯◯◯

DIDYTO
◯◯◯◯◯◯

WELOFL
◯◯◯◯◯◯

I can't believe I was still hungry.

What a large appetite you have.

LITTLE RED RIDING HOOD'S
"GRANDMOTHER" WAS IN
A HURRY TO EAT AND ---

Now arrange the circled letters
to form the surprise answer, as
suggested by the above cartoon.

Print answer here

◯◯◯◯◯◯ ◯◯ ◯◯◯◯

JUMBLE®

Unscramble these four Jumbles, one letter to each square, to form four ordinary words.

DROHC

GEEHD

BLUMME

UBRMEM

This was long overdue. Our customers will be way happier.

They'll sleep like babies.

WHEN THEY REPLACED ALL THE MATTRESSES AT THE HOTEL, IT WAS ---

Now arrange the circled letters to form the surprise answer, as suggested by the above cartoon.

Print answer here

" "

JUMBLE®

Unscramble these four Jumbles, one letter
to each square, to form four ordinary words.

TAYRP

VIHEC

SESUVR

LIFELT

Three strikes away from perfection.

I bet you can hear this crowd 10 miles away.

AT ONE OUT AWAY FROM
A PERFECT GAME, THE
CROWD'S CHEERING
REACHED A ---

Now arrange the circled letters
to form the surprise answer, as
suggested by the above cartoon.

Print
answer
here

JUMBLE®

Unscramble these four Jumbles, one letter
to each square, to form four ordinary words.

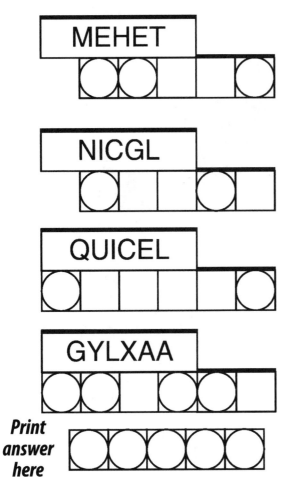

MEHET

NICGL

QUICEL

GYLXAA

Print answer here

This was our winning design from Felix Schlag.

We'll start minting the new nickel right away.

THE BUFFALO NICKEL WAS
REPLACED AFTER THE
MINT APPROVED THE ---

Now arrange the circled letters
to form the surprise answer, as
suggested by the above cartoon.

JUMBLE®

Unscramble these four Jumbles, one letter
to each square, to form four ordinary words.

PXLEE

YPOLO

SUFREE

GJOREG

These glasses will
allow me to focus
near and far?
I don't believe it.

Give them
a try.

BEN FRANKLIN'S
RESPONSE TO BIFOCAL
SKEPTICS WAS ---

Now arrange the circled letters
to form the surprise answer, as
suggested by the above cartoon.

Print answer here

JUMBLE®

Unscramble these four Jumbles, one letter to each square, to form four ordinary words.

MERIG

LOPTI

GADJEG

GNEIOP

A thousand dollars, and you can be hitting the trails in no time.

It needs a lot of work. How about half of that?

Can we get it?

FOR SALE

HE DIDN'T WANT TO PAY MUCH FOR THE OFF-ROAD VEHICLE AND WAS TRYING TO GET IT ---

Now arrange the circled letters to form the surprise answer, as suggested by the above cartoon.

Print answer here ◯◯◯◯ " ◯◯◯◯ "

JUMBLE.

Unscramble these four Jumbles, one letter
to each square, to form four ordinary words.

CNAIP

NTTEH

LBPBEE

RULLAP

This isn't
going to be
easy.

We keep
climbing, no
matter how
difficult.

THEY BUILT THE CASTLE
ON THE HIGHEST POINT
SO THEIR ENEMIES
WOULD HAVE AN ---

Now arrange the circled letters
to form the surprise answer, as
suggested by the above cartoon.

**Print
answer
here**

JUMBLE®

Unscramble these four Jumbles, one letter
to each square, to form four ordinary words.

NUYNS

LOGTA

RODRIT

MTTCOA

THE LANDSCAPERS AT
NASA'S JOHNSON SPACE
CENTER SPECIALIZED IN ---

Now arrange the circled letters
to form the surprise answer, as
suggested by the above cartoon.

*Print
answer
here*

JUMBLE®

Unscramble these four Jumbles, one letter to each square, to form four ordinary words.

NOOEZ

LIYHL

RAURHH

TUNMTO

People like me best because I'm lower in fat.

He's such a ham!

Get a load of his ego.

THE SWISS CHEESE AT THE CHURCH PICNIC HAD AN ATTITUDE THAT WAS ---

Now arrange the circled letters to form the surprise answer, as suggested by the above cartoon.

Print answer here

JUMBLE

Unscramble these four Jumbles, one letter to each square, to form four ordinary words.

HAPTC

ZIYZD

GLIEBR

FUTEFB

Now I see the turn!

I knew it was coming up.

USING THEIR HIGH BEAMS AT NIGHT ON THE UNFAMILIAR ROAD WAS A ---

Now arrange the circled letters to form the surprise answer, as suggested by the above cartoon.

Print answer here

JUMBLE®

Unscramble these four Jumbles, one letter
to each square, to form four ordinary words.

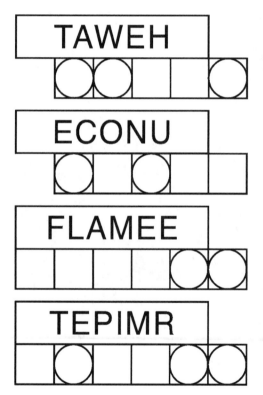

TAWEH

ECONU

FLAMEE

TEPIMR

Head to
the point
at 20 miles
per hour.
Then, take
me to the
course
going 30
miles per
hour.

You're the
boss!

THE SKIER GAVE
EXACT INSTRUCTIONS
AND EXPECTED THE
SPEEDBOAT DRIVER TO ---

Now arrange the circled letters
to form the surprise answer, as
suggested by the above cartoon.

**Print
answer
here**

JUMBLE®

Unscramble these four Jumbles, one letter to each square, to form four ordinary words.

RANGT

LADIP

OPYROL

CRUBHN

I'm writing about my life and my work.

Are you writing a book about cars?

That would be a good title!

THE BOOK ABOUT HENRY FORD AND HIS CAR COMPANY WAS AN ---

Now arrange the circled letters to form the surprise answer, as suggested by the above cartoon.

Print answer here

" ◯◯◯◯ " - ◯◯◯◯◯◯◯◯◯◯

JUMBLE®

Unscramble these four Jumbles, one letter to each square, to form four ordinary words.

WRAPN

LASIA

BRGIEG

SLEUUF

It isn't going anywhere.

The mic is secure?

WHEN THE SPIES SECURELY PLACED THE HIDDEN LISTENING DEVICE, IT WAS ---

Now arrange the circled letters to form the surprise answer, as suggested by the above cartoon.

Print answer here

JUMBLE®

Unscramble these four Jumbles, one letter to each square, to form four ordinary words.

DWNOU

TURET

STOAMC

EYTPRO

Wow!

They are so beautiful!

WHEN THE BALLET SCENE FEATURED A DUO OF BALLERINAS, ALL EYES WERE DRAWN ---

Now arrange the circled letters to form the surprise answer, as suggested by the above cartoon.

Print answer here

JUMBLE®

Unscramble these four Jumbles, one letter to each square, to form four ordinary words.

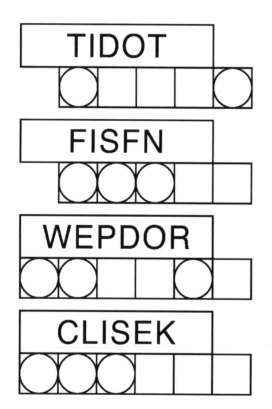

TIDOT

FISFN

WEPDOR

CLISEK

I heard we're coming out with two new flavors.

I heard they're going to make cherry pie and smoked bacon.

THE ICE CREAM SHOP EMPLOYEES KNEW A LOT BECAUSE THEY HAD THE ---

Now arrange the circled letters to form the surprise answer, as suggested by the above cartoon.

Print answer here

JUMBLE®

Unscramble these four Jumbles, one letter to each square, to form four ordinary words.

ZWTAL

BAYTB

OIYICD

ATROHU

She's going to be huge! What's taking her so long?

You took your time, and you were fine.

HER BABY WAS OVERDUE, AND THE EXPECTANT MOM WAS ANXIOUS ABOUT THE ---

Now arrange the circled letters to form the surprise answer, as suggested by the above cartoon.

Print answer here ◯◯◯◯◯ " ◯◯◯◯ "

JUMBLE®

Unscramble these four Jumbles, one letter to each square, to form four ordinary words.

NUBTL

EENFC

PONYCA

OLRALD

We've had another shipment returned.

This is not helping our reputation.

SHODDY WORKMANSHIP AT THE MIRROR FACTORY WAS BEGINNING TO ---

Now arrange the circled letters to form the surprise answer, as suggested by the above cartoon.

Print answer here

JUMBLE®

Unscramble these four Jumbles, one letter to each square, to form four ordinary words.

AALSS

HASOC

DEFARO

RABPUL

This is great! I'm glad it's finally open!

C'mon, Dad! Cannonball!

THE GRAND OPENING OF THE REC CENTER'S NEW POOL ---

Now arrange the circled letters to form the surprise answer, as suggested by the above cartoon.

Print answer here

JUMBLE®

Unscramble these four Jumbles, one letter
to each square, to form four ordinary words.

WNEUD

PRIVE

VGENOR

ARROTO

Hello, ladies, it's
been fun talking to
you. This one is
on the house.

You're
so nice.

THE NEW BARTENDER
GOT TO KNOW HIS
CUSTOMERS BY
ESTABLISHING A ---

Now arrange the circled letters
to form the surprise answer, as
suggested by the above cartoon.

Print
answer
here

JUMBLE®

Unscramble these four Jumbles, one letter
to each square, to form four ordinary words.

BATHI

PHETD

TUBEAN

LTANUW

Well, you're a
great listener!
This is nice
and snug.

It looks just
like yours,
sir!

HE CHECKED THE KNOTS
FOR TIGHTNESS TO SEE
IF THEY'D LEARNED ---

Now arrange the circled letters
to form the surprise answer, as
suggested by the above cartoon.

**Print
answer
here**

JUMBLE

Unscramble these four Jumbles, one letter
to each square, to form four ordinary words.

OOFGR

LSLAT

ROCNUC

CELHKE

THE YOUNG DETECTIVE LED
THE INVESTIGATION UNTIL A
SENIOR DETECTIVE ---

Now arrange the circled letters
to form the surprise answer, as
suggested by the above cartoon.

*Print
answer
here*

JUMBLE®

Unscramble these four Jumbles, one letter
to each square, to form four ordinary words.

LIVAL

DIUTA

DCXEEE

LAIFEN

¿Qué piensas? Do you like it?

España

Was that a gag gift?

It's perfect!

I love it!

WHEN SHE WORE HER
NEW WOOL CHRISTMAS
SWEATER, THE SPANISH
TEACHER SAID ---

Now arrange the circled letters
to form the surprise answer, as
suggested by the above cartoon.

Print
answer
here

" ☐☐☐☐☐☐ " ☐☐☐☐☐☐☐☐

JUMBLE®

Unscramble these four Jumbles, one letter
to each square, to form four ordinary words.

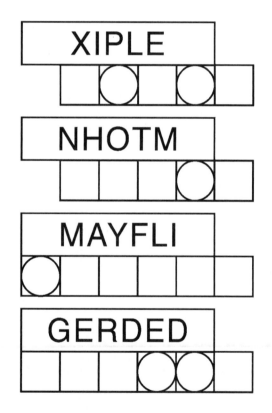

XIPLE

NHOTM

MAYFLI

GERDED

What do we have here?

You are so talented!

They're presents for everyone.

WHEN IT CAME TO MAKING
PRESENTS FOR HER FAMILY,
THE GIRL WAS ---

Now arrange the circled letters
to form the surprise answer, as
suggested by the above cartoon.

Print answer here

JUMBLE®

Unscramble these four Jumbles, one letter
to each square, to form four ordinary words.

DUGEN

WLEDL

BURUNA

LRIFAY

With costs down, we
should raise prices.
Who's in favor?
I could use
another
house.

VOTING TO RAISE PRICES
MORE THAN 500 PERCENT,
THE SELFISH BUSINESS
PEOPLE ---

Now arrange the circled letters
to form the surprise answer, as
suggested by the above cartoon.

Print
answer
here

 "  "

JUMBLE®

Unscramble these four Jumbles, one letter to each square, to form four ordinary words.

CUVOH

CANET

PHISMA

WUDINN

He has no clue.

Hey, toots! How's it going?

We need to talk.

THE TV ANCHORMAN DIDN'T KNOW HE WAS ABOUT TO BE FIRED. IT WOULD SOON BE ---

Now arrange the circled letters to form the surprise answer, as suggested by the above cartoon.

Print answer here

JUMBLE®

Unscramble these four Jumbles, one letter
to each square, to form four ordinary words.

XINEV

MILDY

VRREOF

GRYTEA

Our land can
supply the whole
town with power!

They don't
even affect
our crops.

WHEN THEY INSTALLED
WINDMILLS ON THE FARM,
THEY CREATED AN ---

Now arrange the circled letters
to form the surprise answer, as
suggested by the above cartoon.

Print answer here

JUMBLE®

Unscramble these four Jumbles, one letter to each square, to form four ordinary words.

LECRI

VERNA

TTETAS

LODDEO

It's pretty rusted.

I can't believe this is still standing. —

THE BADLY-DECAYING METAL GATE AT THE OLD MANSION WAS MADE OF ---

Now arrange the circled letters to form the surprise answer, as suggested by the above cartoon.

Print answer here "  "

JUMBLE®

Unscramble these four Jumbles, one letter
to each square, to form four ordinary words.

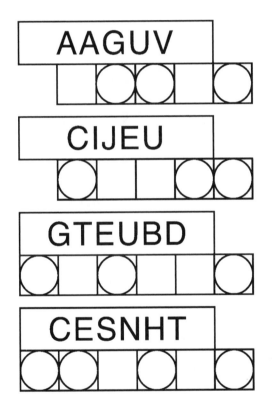

AAGUV

CIJEU

GTEUBD

CESNHT

I like having
the use of
my fingers.

My fingers
stay warmer
in these.

WHETHER OR NOT GLOVES
OR MITTENS ARE BETTER
WAS THE ---

Now arrange the circled letters
to form the surprise answer, as
suggested by the above cartoon.

Print
answer
here

JUMBLE®

Unscramble these four Jumbles, one letter
to each square, to form four ordinary words.

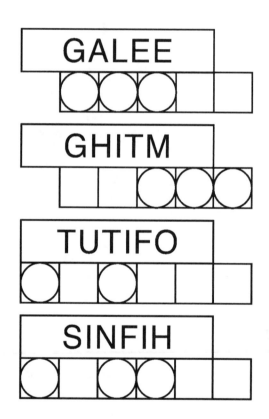

GALEE

GHITM

TUTIFO

SINFIH

I think
this is
the best
one yet.

Yep. I'm
becoming a pro.

THEY'D NEVER PUT UP
WALLPAPER BEFORE. IT
TOOK THEM A WHILE TO ---

Now arrange the circled letters
to form the surprise answer, as
suggested by the above cartoon.

Print
answer
here

 THE

JUMBLE®

Unscramble these four Jumbles, one letter to each square, to form four ordinary words.

FAYCN

OTUBA

MHISPR

GRUBER

We are now ready for the first break.

Now?

THE TELEVISED POOL TOURNAMENT BEGAN ---

Now arrange the circled letters to form the surprise answer, as suggested by the above cartoon.

Print answer here

JUMBLE®

Unscramble these four Jumbles, one letter
to each square, to form four ordinary words.

RTLIF

CEYAD

NRIHUC

PSOOEP

WHEN IT BECAME CLEAR
THEY WERE BREAKING UP,
THE BEATLES WERE ---

Now arrange the circled letters
to form the surprise answer, as
suggested by the above cartoon.

Print answer here ◯◯◯◯ " ◯◯◯◯ "

JUMBLE®

Unscramble these four Jumbles, one letter to each square, to form four ordinary words.

DALNG

HNEEC

LLOGAB

FSMITI

I need to get this jump in to get certified.

Sorry, our mechanic called in sick today and our pilot's late.

THE DELAYS AT THE SKYDIVING SCHOOL WERE A RESULT OF ---

Now arrange the circled letters to form the surprise answer, as suggested by the above cartoon.

Print answer here

JUMBLE®

Unscramble these four Jumbles, one letter to each square, to form four ordinary words.

EGTUS

MNOWA

TINKET

SLOPIH

I knew I smelled something! You said you quit!

HIS ATTEMPT TO GIVE UP CIGARETTES ---

Now arrange the circled letters to form the surprise answer, as suggested by the above cartoon.

Print answer here

JUMBLE®

Unscramble these four Jumbles, one letter
to each square, to form four ordinary words.

ESEGE

GBAYB

DINEDH

NOJRIU

Did either of you pass the bar? You really need to be better prepared in my court.

Yes, Your Honor.

THE LAWYERS IN THE COURTROOM WERE ---

Now arrange the circled letters
to form the surprise answer, as
suggested by the above cartoon.

Print answer here

JUMBLE®

Unscramble these four Jumbles, one letter
to each square, to form four ordinary words.

OAALK

TIYKT

CPCINI

LIFEDD

It goes like, "da dum, da dum, da dum da dum, da dum da dummmmm.."

I love it! How do you do it?

THE THEME FOR THE INSPECTOR CLOUSEAU FILM CAUSED BLAKE EDWARDS TO BE ---

Now arrange the circled letters
to form the surprise answer, as
suggested by the above cartoon.

**Print
answer
here**

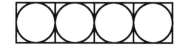

JUMBLE®

Unscramble these four Jumbles, one letter to each square, to form four ordinary words.

SHOEU

RFADT

CURPSE

UNRRNE

You can clearly see these windows are faulty.

I've seen enough! I find for the plaintiffs.

I object?

THE COURT CASE AGAINST THE MANUFACTURER OF THE FAULTY WINDOWS WAS ---

Now arrange the circled letters to form the surprise answer, as suggested by the above cartoon.

Print answer here

JUMBLE®

Unscramble these four Jumbles, one letter
to each square, to form four ordinary words.

AULFW

KIDNR

SEWBOT

XEOPES

Fire! Whoo-hoo!
You guys are the
best scouts!

Wow!
He's
excited.

We better
not let it go
out.

AFTER TEACHING THE
SCOUTS HOW TO BUILD A
CAMPFIRE, THE TROOP
LEADER ---

Now arrange the circled letters
to form the surprise answer, as
suggested by the above cartoon.

*Print answer
here*

JUMBLE®

Unscramble these four Jumbles, one letter to each square, to form four ordinary words.

CIWET

TAMLE

CAGIRL

SIRICS

We'll let people look but not touch. It's amazing!

We need to have a party to show this off.

THE COUPLE WHO HAD THEIR SOFA RE-COVERED WITH A VERY EXPENSIVE FABRIC WERE ---

Now arrange the circled letters to form the surprise answer, as suggested by the above cartoon.

Print answer here

JUMBLE®

Unscramble these four Jumbles, one letter
to each square, to form four ordinary words.

SIBSL

LOTAG

SNLIPT

MARYEC

ONE DAY PEOPLE LIVING IN
ORBIT WILL BE ABLE TO
WATCH TV ON ---

Now arrange the circled letters
to form the surprise answer, as
suggested by the above cartoon.

Print
answer
here

JUMBLE®

Unscramble these four Jumbles, one letter
to each square, to form four ordinary words.

PACRM

TOODU

YORTEH

DEFLID

THE LAWYERS MET
FOR LUNCH AT THE ---

Now arrange the circled letters
to form the surprise answer, as
suggested by the above cartoon.

*Print answer
here*

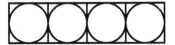

125

JUMBLE®

Unscramble these four Jumbles, one letter to each square, to form four ordinary words.

SUDEO

RYDEB

NASTOA

TNNTIE

This is taking forever.

50% off

I think she's shoplifting.

THE PEOPLE WAITING TO PAY FOR THEIR PURCHASES WERE ---

Now arrange the circled letters to form the surprise answer, as suggested by the above cartoon.

Print answer here "◯◯◯-◯◯◯◯◯◯◯◯◯"

JUMBLE®

Unscramble these four Jumbles, one letter
to each square, to form four ordinary words.

CIBHR

GRIET

SDWHER

ONWWID

THEIR NEW TALKING
SCALE HAD A ---

Now arrange the circled letters
to form the surprise answer, as
suggested by the above cartoon.

Print answer here

"⬡⬡⬡⬡⬡" ⬡⬡⬡⬡ ⬡⬡⬡⬡⬡⬡

JUMBLE®

Unscramble these four Jumbles, one letter
to each square, to form four ordinary words.

KNIDE

TPEGU

ARTNUT

LCIHNF

Me too?

I think this has
mowed its last
lawn.

IT WAS TIME TO GET A NEW
LAWN MOWER BECAUSE THE
ONE THEY HAD WASN'T ---

Now arrange the circled letters
to form the surprise answer, as
suggested by the above cartoon.

**Print answer
here**

128

JUMBLE®

Unscramble these four Jumbles, one letter to each square, to form four ordinary words.

DMTIS

CNUHM

DNRWIA

NOCROB

We left our phones at home.

We don't want to be disturbed.

No one is going to bother you up here.

THE REMOTE BED AND BREAKFAST ALLOWED THE NEWLYWEDS TO BE ---

Now arrange the circled letters to form the surprise answer, as suggested by the above cartoon.

Print answer here

" ☐☐☐ - ☐☐☐☐☐☐☐☐☐☐ "

JUMBLE®

Unscramble these four Jumbles, one letter
to each square, to form four ordinary words.

KIRBE

YEXPO

EFYLER

GELHIS

They should
fit you
perfectly
now.

They look great.
I'll wear them
out.

HER NEW GLASSES WERE
READY AND WERE RIGHT ---

Now arrange the circled letters
to form the surprise answer, as
suggested by the above cartoon.

**Print
answer
here**   " ◯◯ - ◯◯◯ " ◯◯◯ ◯◯◯◯

JUMBLE®

Unscramble these four Jumbles, one letter
to each square, to form four ordinary words.

DONMU

TUCHH

YNITLH

QAEOUP

I need you to take care of these things before I get home in an hour.

I was going out back with the guys.

THE KANGAROO GAVE HER HUSBAND A TO-DO LIST AND EXPECTED HIM TO ---

Now arrange the circled letters
to form the surprise answer, as
suggested by the above cartoon.

Print answer here

JUMBLE®

Unscramble these four Jumbles, one letter
to each square, to form four ordinary words.

LUTPI

BWALY

IUCSCR

DENDDO

It looks pretty
simple. Slice thin,
season, then
place on racks.

I knew it was
straightforward.

THE PROCESS FOR
MAKING BEEF
JERKY IS ---

Now arrange the circled letters
to form the surprise answer, as
suggested by the above cartoon.

*Print answer
here*

JUMBLE®

Unscramble these four Jumbles, one letter to each square, to form four ordinary words.

WOYSN

CEOGK

SARPIN

SHRUOC

We did it!

I kind of like my meat raw.

Arrrrrr!

Yes, "we" did.

WHEN THE LIONS FIGURED OUT HOW TO BUILD A FIRE, IT WAS A ---

Now arrange the circled letters to form the surprise answer, as suggested by the above cartoon.

Print answer here

JUMBLE®

Unscramble these four Jumbles, one letter
to each square, to form four ordinary words.

ONWSO

VODTI

HRYITT

SAUCCE

I feel I've
done it all
before.

Have you
tried props?
How about
impersonations?

WHEN THE STAND-UP
COMEDIAN RAN OUT OF
NEW IDEAS, HE WAS ---

Now arrange the circled letters
to form the surprise answer, as
suggested by the above cartoon.

Print
answer
here

JUMBLE®

Unscramble these four Jumbles, one letter
to each square, to form four ordinary words.

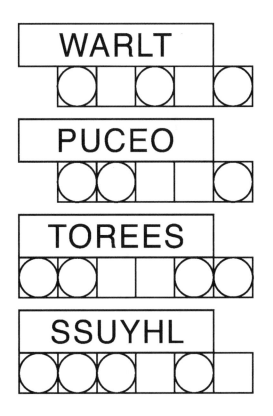

WARLT

PUCEO

TOREES

SSUYHL

THE BOUTIQUE WAS
GOING OUT OF BUSINESS,
SO THEY HAD A ---

Now arrange the circled letters
to form the surprise answer, as
suggested by the above cartoon.

*Print
answer
here*

" ◯◯◯◯◯◯◯-◯◯◯ " ◯◯◯◯◯

JUMBLE®

Unscramble these four Jumbles, one letter
to each square, to form four ordinary words.

DEMMO

KEHRI

TAYRIF

CEJERT

Are you
coming to
the opera?

I'm going
to spend
a few
more
hours on
my clock.

WILLIAM CLEMENT INVENTED
THE GRANDFATHER CLOCK
BECAUSE HE WAS ABLE TO ---

Now arrange the circled letters
to form the surprise answer, as
suggested by the above cartoon.

Print
answer
here

JUMBLE®

Unscramble these four Jumbles, one letter to each square, to form four ordinary words.

RAYHI

HTALC

WLATLE

CEFOFE

I can't even relate to what you're saying.

Wow! That was a great drive.

I love the feel of dirt on my treads.

Yep! What a great ride.

THE SPARE DIDN'T ALWAYS FIT IN WITH THE OTHER FOUR TIRES AND OFTEN FELT LIKE A ---

Now arrange the circled letters to form the surprise answer, as suggested by the above cartoon.

Print answer here

JUMBLE®

Unscramble these four Jumbles, one letter to each square, to form four ordinary words.

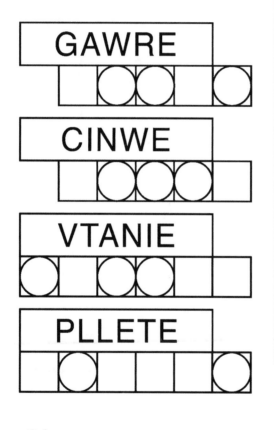

GAWRE

CINWE

VTANIE

PLLETE

But soft, what light through yonder window breaks? It is the east, and Juliet is the sun.

Whatever.

Did you two break up again? In this play, you're supposed to be in love!

THE STAGE PERFORMERS OFTEN HAD PROBLEMS ---

Now arrange the circled letters to form the surprise answer, as suggested by the above cartoon.

Print answer here

JUMBLE®

Unscramble these four Jumbles, one letter
to each square, to form four ordinary words.

OGYOE

SAHHR

WTREET

ANNPIK

Is that a new
song you're
writing?

Nah. I'm just
playing
around
with some
chords.

THE GUITARIST CAME UP
WITH A NEW MELODY, BUT
DIDN'T THINK IT WAS ---

Now arrange the circled letters
to form the surprise answer, as
suggested by the above cartoon.

**Print
answer
here**

JUMBLE®

Unscramble these four Jumbles, one letter to each square, to form four ordinary words.

NYIKD

NORGP

INCSEK

LAEVBI

Don't be shy. Let me see those beautiful golden scales.

I don't think so.

THE CARP THAT HID BEHIND THE ROCK IN THE GARDEN POOL WAS ---

Now arrange the circled letters to form the surprise answer, as suggested by the above cartoon.

Print answer here ◯◯◯◯◯ " ◯◯◯ "

JUMBLE®

Unscramble these four Jumbles, one letter
to each square, to form four ordinary words.

GEMOA

PWRIE

DNOENC

ITRIED

I can do Monday at
either nine or 10.

Nine's
too early.
Let's do
10 o'clock.

THEY WANTED TO
GO BOWLING. THEY
JUST NEEDED TO ---

Now arrange the circled letters
to form the surprise answer, as
suggested by the above cartoon.

*Print
answer
here*

JUMBLE®

Unscramble these four Jumbles, one letter to each square, to form four ordinary words.

AFROV

NRTKU

SUMSIE

LETWAH

How does the mommy know what to do?

She just does.

THE DEER GAVE BIRTH AND KNEW WHAT TO DO THANKS TO HER ---

Now arrange the circled letters to form the surprise answer, as suggested by the above cartoon.

Print answer here

JUMBLE®

Unscramble these four Jumbles, one letter
to each square, to form four ordinary words.

SUYBH

POGUR

RUYTTS

GRIEHH

They've always gotten along so well. No wonder they succeeded.

They did it!

Most family members wouldn't survive such an endeavor.

FOR AMERICA TO BECOME A PIONEER IN THE AVIATION INDUSTRY, IT TOOK THE ---

Now arrange the circled letters
to form the surprise answer, as
suggested by the above cartoon.

Print answer here " ⃝⃝⃝⃝⃝ " ⃝⃝⃝⃝⃝⃝⃝⃝⃝

JUMBLE®

Unscramble these four Jumbles, one letter
to each square, to form four ordinary words.

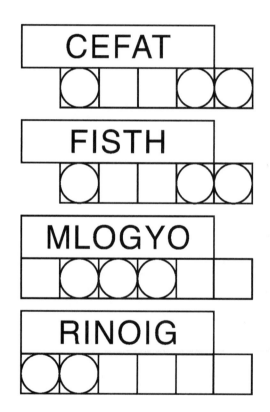

CEFAT

FISTH

MLOGYO

RINOIG

THE SUBDIVISION WHERE
THEY CHOSE TO BUILD THEIR
DREAM HOME HAD ---

Now arrange the circled letters
to form the surprise answer, as
suggested by the above cartoon.

**Print
answer
here**

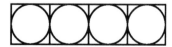 

JUMBLE®

Unscramble these four Jumbles, one letter
to each square, to form four ordinary words.

TAKEW

RSUBT

DOGRUN

SIYEFT

I ran here with
our patent!

Fantastic!
Let's step up
our production.

AFTER RECEIVING A PATENT
FOR THE RUBBER HEEL,
HUMPHREY O'SULLIVAN MADE ---

Now arrange the circled letters
to form the surprise answer, as
suggested by the above cartoon.

Print
answer
here

JUMBLE®

Unscramble these four Jumbles, one letter
to each square, to form four ordinary words.

MWASP

GUYNO

NUTIDC

ARMCEA

We'll be able to
travel even
when the
winds are not
in our favor.

We'll be
able to
reach farther
distances
too.

THE NEW HUMAN-POWERED
GREEK SHIP WOULD BE ABLE
TO STAY AT SEA FOR ---

Now arrange the circled letters
to form the surprise answer, as
suggested by the above cartoon.

**Print
answer
here**

JUMBLE®

Unscramble these four Jumbles, one letter
to each square, to form four ordinary words.

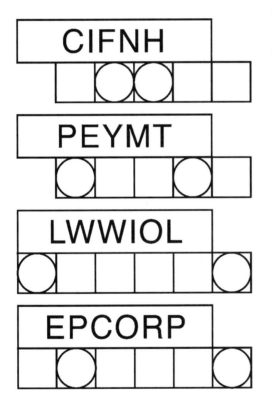

CIFNH

PEYMT

LWWIOL

EPCORP

Are you ready to go?

Sorry. I have a great story idea that I have to start on before I forget.

HE NEEDED TO GET STARTED
ON HIS NEW NOVEL AND
WOULD BEGIN ---

Now arrange the circled letters
to form the surprise answer, as
suggested by the above cartoon.

Print answer here

JUMBLE®

Unscramble these four Jumbles, one letter to each square, to form four ordinary words.

POMHO

LEYID

YALVEL

EEWIDV

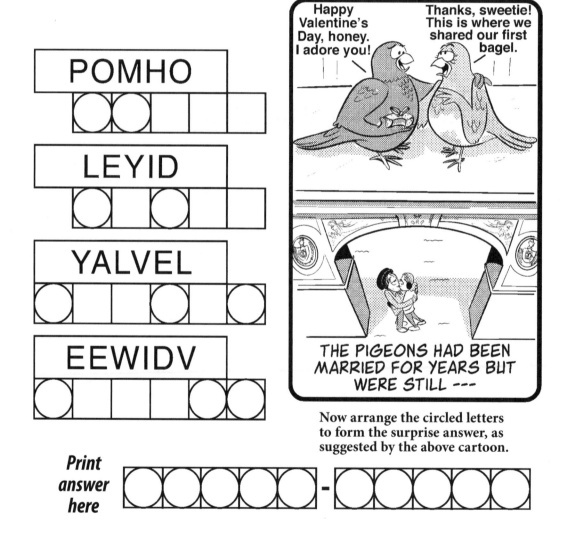

Happy Valentine's Day, honey. I adore you!

Thanks, sweetie! This is where we shared our first bagel.

THE PIGEONS HAD BEEN MARRIED FOR YEARS BUT WERE STILL ---

Now arrange the circled letters to form the surprise answer, as suggested by the above cartoon.

Print answer here

◯◯◯◯◯ - ◯◯◯◯◯

JUMBLE®

Unscramble these four Jumbles, one letter
to each square, to form four ordinary words.

HTISF

TOPOH

ACCSTU

LEEUFY

We are now going
live to a police
pursuit of a
stolen truck.

WHEN THE ANCHORMAN WAS
TOLD THERE WAS A PURSUIT
IN PROGRESS, HE ---

Now arrange the circled letters
to form the surprise answer, as
suggested by the above cartoon.

Print
answer
here

JUMBLE®

Unscramble these four Jumbles, one letter to each square, to form four ordinary words.

ZEIES

BNARD

RSHOCC

QUPALE

We're late because of them.

They're so rude!

Sir, you need to shut off your phone.

— In a minute.

THE FLIGHT ATTENDANTS WERE UNDER A LOT OF STRESS AND WERE FEELING THE ---

Now arrange the circled letters to form the surprise answer, as suggested by the above cartoon.

Print answer here

JUMBLE®

Unscramble these four Jumbles, one letter to each square, to form four ordinary words.

VOREG

RHEBT

SRLIPA

RANWID

We need to take some tricks, Fran.

I love playing here.

We've got this, Mom.

WHEN THEY PLAYED CARDS IN VIEW OF THE GOLDEN GATE, THEY WERE ---

Now arrange the circled letters to form the surprise answer, as suggested by the above cartoon.

Print answer here

JUMBLE®

Unscramble these four Jumbles, one letter to each square, to form four ordinary words.

RIOVS

CATTR

GILWEG

EESWFT

A long time ago in a galaxy far, far away....

This movie is so great!

Luke is my favorite!

I've seen it three times.

MANY PEOPLE SAW "STAR WARS" MULTIPLE TIMES AND GAVE IT ---

Now arrange the circled letters to form the surprise answer, as suggested by the above cartoon.

Print answer here

"☐☐-☐☐☐☐☐"

JUMBLE®

Unscramble these four Jumbles, one letter
to each square, to form four ordinary words.

ATBEA

SEMYS

CNECTA

KMIYSP

You're a lifesaver! How do you do it so quickly?

I used to work in an alteration shop.

SHE COULD HAND-SEW
A HEM VERY QUICKLY
AND MADE IT ---

Now arrange the circled letters
to form the surprise answer, as
suggested by the above cartoon.

Print answer here " ◯◯◯◯ " ◯◯◯◯

JUMBLE®

Unscramble these four Jumbles, one letter
to each square, to form four ordinary words.

LENTK

ROMBO

CNIESC

IROADH

So, what do you think?

You're a genius!

THE TOLL HOUSE INN'S
RUTH WAKEFIELD, THE
CREATOR OF CHOCOLATE
CHIPS, WAS ---

Now arrange the circled letters
to form the surprise answer, as
suggested by the above cartoon.

Print
answer
here

JUMBLE®

Unscramble these four Jumbles, one letter
to each square, to form four ordinary words.

TUYPT

HEWLE

CEINTE

EFOTEF

You have nothing
to worry about.
You and your
mare will be the
talk of the barn
dance.

I don't
want to
embarrass
her.

THE HORSE WANTED TO TAKE
DANCING LESSONS BUT WAS
WORRIED ABOUT HIS ---

Now arrange the circled letters
to form the surprise answer, as
suggested by the above cartoon.

*Print
answer
here*

JUMBLE®

Unscramble these four Jumbles, one letter
to each square, to form four ordinary words.

NOYIR

INAPO

GDYALL

MLUTEB

WHEN THE TRACK COACH'S
STOPWATCH WOULDN'T
WORK, IT WAS ---

Now arrange the circled letters
to form the surprise answer, as
suggested by the above cartoon.

*Print
answer
here*

JUMBLE®

Unscramble these four Jumbles, one letter
to each square, to form four ordinary words.

NALUN

USENE

TRIGYT

RUVEDO

This is the
second time
this week that
it's stopped
working! You
need to fix this
immediately!

It's still
cold air.

WHEN THEIR BRAND-NEW
HEATING/COOLING SYSTEM
BROKE AGAIN, HE ---

Now arrange the circled letters
to form the surprise answer, as
suggested by the above cartoon.

Print
answer
here

⬡⬡⬡⬡⬡⬡ HIS ⬡⬡⬡⬡⬡

JUMBLE®

Unscramble these four Jumbles, one letter
to each square, to form four ordinary words.

NUDHO

BBIER

OIDING

RGYGOG

You all are so precious!

I'm off to work.

Mama!

Don't ever put me down.

I'm hungry.

Can I go to work too?

Mama!

THE ANT'S EGGS HATCHED,
AND SHE DIDN'T MIND A BIT
WHEN THE BABIES STARTED ---

Now arrange the circled letters
to form the surprise answer, as
suggested by the above cartoon.

Print
answer
here

JUMBLE®

Unscramble these four Jumbles, one letter
to each square, to form four ordinary words.

RYDTI

KMISP

NEETTX

CCHITE

Morning!
How 'bout a
kiss?

Go take
a shower,
now!

HER HUSBAND SMELLED
HORRIBLE AFTER HIS
SWEATY WORKOUT, SO
SHE GAVE HIM THE ---

Now arrange the circled letters
to form the surprise answer, as
suggested by the above cartoon.

Print answer here

JUMBLE®

Unscramble these four Jumbles, one letter to each square, to form four ordinary words.

VRFEE

SOEBE

SOLIRA

TONEMM

BETWEEN THE BALTIC AND THE MEDITERRANEAN, THEY VISITED SITES ---

Now arrange the circled letters to form the surprise answer, as suggested by the above cartoon.

Print answer here

JUMBLE®

Unscramble these four Jumbles, one letter to each square, to form four ordinary words.

KLUSL

DBEIA

GROEGJ

SLENET

Everyone at work was talking about this show.

I want to work for Eliot Ness!

Gotta go. The show's starting.

WHEN "THE UNTOUCHABLES" BEGAN AIRING IN 1959, VIEWERS TUNED IN ---

Now arrange the circled letters to form the surprise answer, as suggested by the above cartoon.

Print answer here

JUMBLE®

Unscramble these four Jumbles, one letter
to each square, to form four ordinary words.

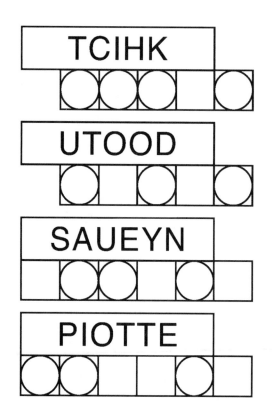

TCIHK

UTOOD

SAUEYN

PIOTTE

I hope you love her
as much as we did.

It just needs a
good cleaning.

I love
this car!

HER GRANDPARENTS
GAVE HER THEIR OLD CAR,
AND SHE REALLY ---

Now arrange the circled letters
to form the surprise answer, as
suggested by the above cartoon.

**Print
answer
here**

A

JUMBLE Christmas

Challenger Puzzles

JUMBLE®

Unscramble these six Jumbles, one letter to each square, to form six ordinary words.

CUPSAM

HASFIM

ROQUIL

TIPECK

KATEIN

DRIVET

STATE U. SCHOOL OF FABRICS

HE HOPED TO MAKE LOTS OF MONEY IN TEXTILES BECAUSE HE WAS INCLINED TO BE THIS.

Now arrange the circled letters to form the surprise answer, as suggested by the above cartoon.

Print answer here

JUMBLE®

Unscramble these six Jumbles, one letter to each square, to form six ordinary words.

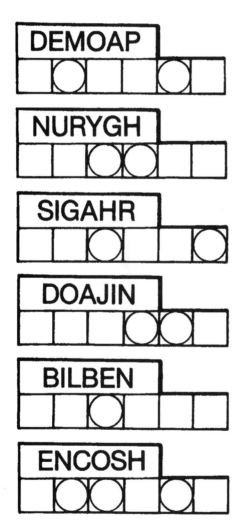

DEMOAP

NURYGH

SIGAHR

DOAJIN

BILBEN

ENCOSH

There goes the environment!

WHAT THEY CALLED THE GANGSTER WHO MOVED NEXT DOOR.

Now arrange the circled letters to form the surprise answer, as suggested by the above cartoon.

Print answer here

THE "  "

JUMBLE®

Unscramble these six Jumbles, one letter
to each square, to form six ordinary words.

MOYPLE

SICCEN

NAANAB

TRUGET

CAVELE

EMSIDE

THE FIRST DUTY OF
THE MISSIONARY WAS
TO CONVERT THE
CANNIBALS TO THIS.

Now arrange the circled letters
to form the surprise answer, as
suggested by the above cartoon.

Print answer here

166

JUMBLE®

Unscramble these six Jumbles, one letter to each square, to form six ordinary words.

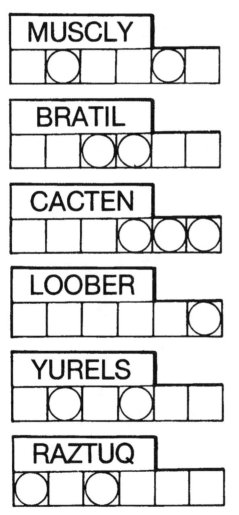

MUSCLY

BRATIL

CACTEN

LOOBER

YURELS

RAZTUQ

THE KIND OF PEOPLE YOU MIGHT MEET AT THE INFOR- MATION BUREAU.

Now arrange the circled letters to form the surprise answer, as suggested by the above cartoon.

Print answer here

" " ONES

JUMBLE®

Unscramble these six Jumbles, one letter to each square, to form six ordinary words.

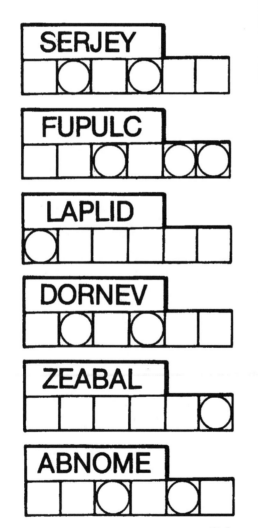

SERJEY

FUPULC

LAPLID

DORNEV

ZEABAL

ABNOME

This should get him to make up his mind

POST OFFICE

You're right, Mom

WHAT THAT LOVE LETTER WAS CALCULATED TO DO.

Now arrange the circled letters to form the surprise answer, as suggested by the above cartoon.

Print answer here

◯◯◯◯◯ ◯◯ THE "◯◯◯◯"

JUMBLE®

Unscramble these six Jumbles, one letter
to each square, to form six ordinary words.

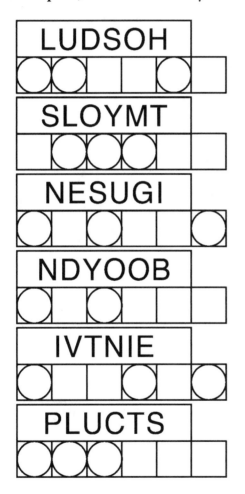

LUDSOH

SLOYMT

NESUGI

NDYOOB

IVTNIE

PLUCTS

The profits have
really added up. I
have a new house
and a new chariot.

Your
abacuses are
everywhere.

Welcome to the
Abacus Store.

Here
we've
upgraded
the beads.

THE ABACUS SELLER'S
BUSINESS HAD PROSPERED
WHICH ALLOWED HIM TO ---

Now arrange the circled letters
to form the surprise answer, as
suggested by the above cartoon.

Print answer here

JUMBLE®

Unscramble these six Jumbles, one letter to each square, to form six ordinary words.

HCTTAH

EYULSR

FIRTAF

BRANER

MITGAB

BACLOT

Is there a problem with the check, sir?

Are you feeling all right, honey?

Whoa! It's so much! How did it get so big?

THE MEAL AT THE FANCY RESTAURANT WAS DELICIOUS, BUT THEY WERE HAVING PROBLEMS ---

Now arrange the circled letters to form the surprise answer, as suggested by the above cartoon.

Print answer here

JUMBLE®

Unscramble these six Jumbles, one letter to each square, to form six ordinary words.

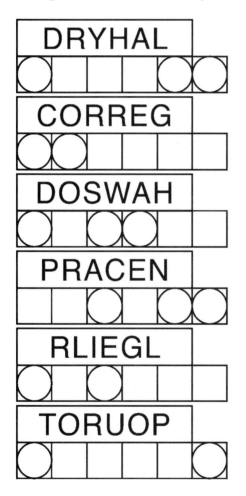

DRYHAL

CORREG

DOSWAH

PRACEN

RLIEGL

TORUOP

You've been caught red-handed. Do you have anything to say before I sentence you?

I was framed.

THE THIEF WHO STOLE CREDIT CARD NUMBERS AND USED THEM TO MAKE PURCHASES WAS ---

Now arrange the circled letters to form the surprise answer, as suggested by the above cartoon.

Print answer here

JUMBLE®

Unscramble these six Jumbles, one letter to each square, to form six ordinary words.

TURFHO

PAXNED

CRONEE

AARRUO

RTRWIE

MULVEO

This is great! It's nice to not have the Union Jack on our flag anymore.

This is such a positive day for us!

Wow!

WHEN CANADA REPLACED ITS FLAG IN 1965 WITH ITS CURRENT FLAG, THEY ---

Now arrange the circled letters to form the surprise answer, as suggested by the above cartoon.

Print answer here

◯◯◯◯◯◯ ◯◯◯◯◯ A ◯◯◯◯ ◯◯◯◯

JUMBLE®

Unscramble these six Jumbles, one letter
to each square, to form six ordinary words.

GAITMS

SPOGSI

GRIHAS

FRUUET

LUTEML

TRYHOW

THE COMPUTER CODER
WANTED HIS LAZY
CO-WORKER TO ---

Now arrange the circled letters
to form the surprise answer, as
suggested by the above cartoon.

Print answer here

JUMBLE®

Unscramble these six Jumbles, one letter to each square, to form six ordinary words.

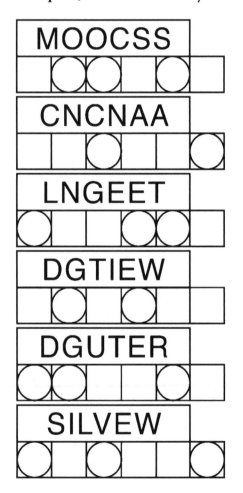

MOOCSS

CNCNAA

LNGEET

DGTIEW

DGUTER

SILVEW

My family has been training here for generations.

It keeps on getting bigger.

CALIFORNIA'S FAMOUS "MUSCLE BEACH" OUTDOOR GYM STARTED IN 1934 AND IS ---

Now arrange the circled letters to form the surprise answer, as suggested by the above cartoon.

Print answer here

JUMBLE®

Unscramble these six Jumbles, one letter to each square, to form six ordinary words.

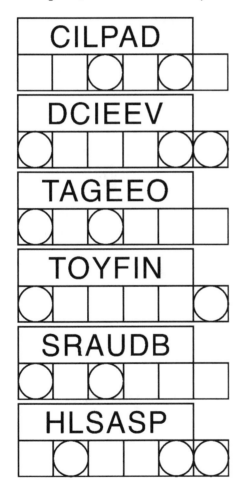

CILPAD

DCIEEV

TAGEEO

TOYFIN

SRAUDB

HLSASP

Is your QB ready for the big game?

His arm has improved every game, and he's had a great week of practice.

Nice throw!

16

THE QUARTERBACK'S PERFORMANCE WAS IMPROVING WITH ---

Now arrange the circled letters to form the surprise answer, as suggested by the above cartoon.

Print answer here

JUMBLE®

Unscramble these six Jumbles, one letter to each square, to form six ordinary words.

CAMTIP

TECDAH

NALFUT

DOYWSO

NROYER

SAWLEE

I need new work gloves.

I can help you right here.

These fit you like a glove.

You're right.

You all are so helpful!

We're here to help.

THE STORE ONLY SOLD GLOVES, MITTENS AND SHOES, AND CUSTOMERS WERE ---

Now arrange the circled letters to form the surprise answer, as suggested by the above cartoon.

Print answer here

⬡⬡⬡⬡⬡⬡ ⬡⬡ ⬡⬡⬡⬡ **AND** ⬡⬡⬡⬡

JUMBLE®

Unscramble these six Jumbles, one letter
to each square, to form six ordinary words.

WRCEUF

OREKBR

KALECC

OMHOCS

GTONTE

ALWWLO

I am not putting that on!

But this is what we're shooting today.

I'm through with her. Send her home.

She's such a prima donna.

THE FASHION MODEL
REFUSED TO TRY
ON ANYTHING AND
WOULD SOON ---

Now arrange the circled letters
to form the surprise answer, as
suggested by the above cartoon.

Print answer here

JUMBLE®

Unscramble these six Jumbles, one letter to each square, to form six ordinary words.

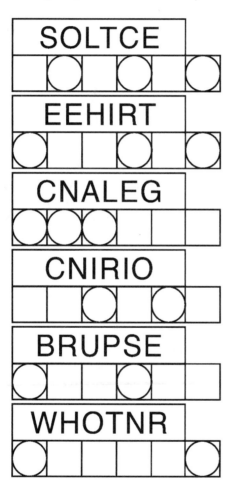

SOLTCE

EEHIRT

CNALEG

CNIRIO

BRUPSE

WHOTNR

You know, we can buy you new jeans.

Yep. I think these may have fallen apart sooner than I thought.

I thought that was the style.

HER JEANS HAD WORN OUT AND WERE ---

Now arrange the circled letters to form the surprise answer, as suggested by the above cartoon.

Print answer here

JUMBLE®

Unscramble these six Jumbles, one letter
to each square, to form six ordinary words.

LEEAWS

LANFUT

HURNCC

EEIDLY

CNEEMA

SALYCS

Are you heading back on the return, or are you staying in L.A.?

Do you ever get airsick?

You get used to it.

Two more hours on this flight, and then I'm done.

THE DISTANCE BETWEEN NYC AND L.A. IN A PASSENGER JET IS 2,500 MILES ---

Now arrange the circled letters
to form the surprise answer, as
suggested by the above cartoon.

Print answer here

JUMBLE®

Unscramble these six Jumbles, one letter to each square, to form six ordinary words.

YFORTS

VETDNA

SWACEH

EDREGE

TIEUYQ

CHIPUC

Oh my gosh! Did I win?

Looks like it. I've been selling a ton of these. They're really taking off.

I'll take one of those!

THE SUCCESSFUL LAUNCH OF THE FIRST INSTANT LOTTERY TICKETS JUST ---

Now arrange the circled letters to form the surprise answer, as suggested by the above cartoon.

Print answer here

⚪⚪⚪⚪⚪⚪⚪⚪⚪ THE ⚪⚪⚪⚪⚪⚪⚪

JUMBLE®

Unscramble these six Jumbles, one letter to each square, to form six ordinary words.

VIQRUE

ENAPTU

RANYEL

FIDAAR

DAALIR

HOEYRT

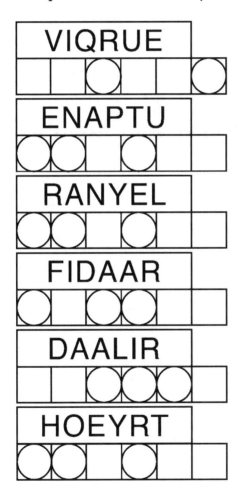

I hope we get this in.

happy ST. PATRICK'S DA

The wind's really picking up.

THE ST. PATRICK'S DAY FESTIVITIES WERE READY TO BEGIN, BUT THEY HOPED IT WOULDN'T ---

Now arrange the circled letters to form the surprise answer, as suggested by the above cartoon.

Print answer here

JUMBLE®

Unscramble these six Jumbles, one letter to each square, to form six ordinary words.

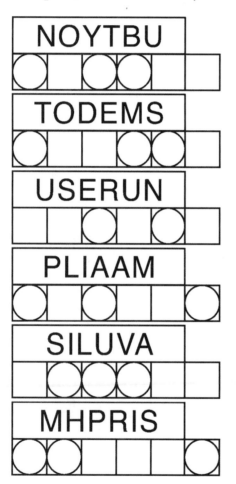

NOYTBU

TODEMS

USERUN

PLIAAM

SILUVA

MHPRIS

That was great! Now we start jumping busses! Maybe a building?

Next, you'll have me jumping the Grand Canyon.

AFTER EVEL KNIEVEL'S EARLY SUCCESS PERFORMING MOTORCYCLE JUMPS, HE WAS ABLE TO ---

Now arrange the circled letters to form the surprise answer, as suggested by the above cartoon.

Print answer here

JUMBLE®

Unscramble these six Jumbles, one letter to each square, to form six ordinary words.

CIPMTA

LNEENF

BHAYSB

SIOACF

LOFARL

GSITTH

I know we're new, but we've got to increase production.

BOEING BECAME A HUGE AIRPLANE MANUFACTURER AFTER GETTING ---

Now arrange the circled letters to form the surprise answer, as suggested by the above cartoon.

Print answer here

Answers

1. **Jumbles:** EVENT BALMY LEGUME POPLIN
Answer: When adding machines were first introduced they were so successful that they began to do this—"MULTIPLY"

2. **Jumbles:** LATCH ADAGE TRAGIC DEVOUR
Answer: She said he was her pet project which must be why she tried to do this—TREAT HIM LIKE A DOG

3. **Jumbles:** AIDED CRAZY RANCID EXCITE
Answer: What they did when that man fell off the horse—"DE-RIDED" HIM

4. **Jumbles:** PHOTO BALKY CATTLE JAILED
Answer: They called that eccentric inventor a crackpot until he did this—HIT THE JACKPOT

5. **Jumbles:** SOAPY FRAME ROSARY BOUNCE
Answer: Do zombies like being dead?—"OF CORPSE"

6. **Jumbles:** POUND BOUGH FERVID TALKER
Answer: What caused the puncture in the tire?—A FORK IN THE ROAD

7. **Jumbles:** SMOKY DAISY FROSTY UPLIFT
Answer: What ice is—"SKID" STUFF

8. **Jumbles:** TACKY FENCE COOKIE SHREWD
Answer: He wore a plaid vest in order to keep this—A CHECK ON HIS WAIST

9. **Jumbles:** TESTY VIXEN LIKELY EASILY
Answer: What liars do after they die—LIE STILL

10. **Jumbles:** AFIRE CROAK POETRY SHOULD
Answer: Would you believe a painter who did this?—SPREAD IT ON THICK

11. **Jumbles:** CROWN EMPTY JUNKET DAWNED
Answer: What the wolf who was going to join the card game brought with him—HIS OWN "PACK"

12. **Jumbles:** LOUSE TIGER PITIED MURMUR
Answer: What the sad tree said after the axman did his work—"I'M STUMPED"

13. **Jumbles:** STOOP CLOTH RADIAL HUNGRY
Answer: A fabulously successful baker might bring these words to mind—ROLLS IN DOUGH

14. **Jumbles:** POISE SUITE HUNTER GHETTO
Answer: Sometimes the real hero of the movie is the one who does this—SITS THROUGH IT

15. **Jumbles:** DANDY FLOUR CATNIP OCCULT
Answer: What the guy who constantly drank hot chocolate must have been—A "COCOA NUT"

16. **Jumbles:** FAULT BROIL FLABBY MEASLY
Answer: When is a boat the cheapest?—WHEN IT'S A "SALE" BOAT

17. **Jumbles:** FLUID HOUSE OPPOSE SQUALL
Answer: What the female dinosaur said to her grouchy mate—YOU OLD FOSSIL

18. **Jumbles:** TWINE NAIVE EYELET MISUSE
Answer: The crowd did this when the winning team passed by—LET OFF "ESTEEM"

19. **Jumbles:** VIRUS FINAL HANSOM UNSAID
Answer: What the city required in order to clean up the aftermath of a big snowstorm—A "SLUSH" FUND

20. **Jumbles:** HUMID PIPER ENTITY MYSELF
Answer: Fat is the penalty for exceeding this—THE FEED LIMIT

21. **Jumbles:** PIKER ADULT MUSEUM PURVEY
Answer: What they called that great magician—A SUPER "DUPER"

22. **Jumbles:** PARCH CHASM BAZAAR HELIUM
Answer: Another name for rabbit fur—HARE HAIR

23. **Jumbles:** HURRY POKER IGUANA SUBTLY
Answer: What the lamebrain said when his lawyer told him he had lost his suit—I'LL BUY ANOTHER

24. **Jumbles:** HOIST APART STIGMA POTTER
Answer: What many a night spot is—A "TIGHT" SPOT

25. **Jumbles:** VAPOR CABLE HANDED FECUND
Answer: The secret agent was always blowing his nose because he had this—A "CODE" IN THE HEAD

26. **Jumbles:** CROWN EXILE JAGGED VORTEX
Answer: They went to that island for "tea" because it was in the middle of this—"WA-T-ER"

27. **Jumbles:** FEINT EXCEL WAITER ASTHMA
Answer: What the sign on the sales lot for mobile homes said—"WHEEL" ESTATE

28. **Jumbles:** LITHE COLIC SPLICE ASTRAY
Answer: What kind of animal helps chase outlaws?—A "POSSE" CAT (pussycat)

29. **Jumbles:** ORBIT LAPEL MORTAR TERROR
Answer: If you're dissatisfied with the color of your hair, a good dye should get to this—THE ROOT OF THE MATTER

30. **Jumbles:** TABOO VALET LOUNGE FROSTY
Answer: Before your diet can flatter you, it must do this—FLATTEN YOU

31. **Jumbles:** ARRAY HAVOC NEEDLE JOCKEY
Answer: Why it's so easy to milk a cow—ANY "JERK" CAN DO IT

32. **Jumbles:** MADAM QUOTA SYMBOL FIERCE
Answer: What the potter was noted for—HIS "FEATS" OF CLAY

33. **Jumbles:** DECAY PRUNE JANGLE AGHAST
Answer: Why everyone loves a banana—IT HAS "A PEEL" (appeal)

34. **Jumbles:** LADLE BRIAR CATCHY TURGID
Answer: You wouldn't want this in a cemetery—TO BE CAUGHT DEAD

35. **Jumbles:** VITAL WHEAT FOSSIL RENDER
Answer: What an airline might do in order to drum up business—HAND OUT "FLIERS"

36. **Jumbles:** NOBLE DAILY FRIEZE CATNIP
Answer: What happens when two egotists have a falling out—IT'S AN "I" FOR AN "I"

37. **Jumbles:** MOUSE AVAIL VOYAGE NAUSEA
Answer: She's determined to do this, no matter how much it costs—SAVE MONEY

38. **Jumbles:** SURLY ENSUE LEGACY PARISH
Answer: What did they call the team made up of Frankenstein monsters?—THE "ALL-SCARS"

39. **Jumbles:** ESSAY AZURE TOUCHY LEDGER
Answer: He makes a monkey of himself whenever he tries to do this—CARRY A "TALE"

40. **Jumbles:** EMPTY AROMA PENCIL SMOKER
Answer: Why the worms didn't enter Noah's ark in "pairs"—THEY CAME IN APPLES

41. **Jumbles:** BROIL ONION ALWAYS BOUNTY
Answer: How it was crossed by a robot—BY A ROWBOAT

42. **Jumbles:** MINOR TIGER GARISH PICKET
Answer: What she said about their new house that looked like a matchbox—IT'S "STRIKING"

43. **Jumbles:** TANGY SHOWY LIQUOR CATTLE
Answer: What happened when the left half of the cake disappeared?—IT WAS "ALL RIGHT"

44. **Jumbles:** VALVE FIFTY BECALM DENTAL
Answer: When he lost his keys and couldn't get in, he ran around the house until he was this—ALL "IN"

45. **Jumbles:** MANLY HAZEL PARLOR SNAPPY
Answer: What that popular chef corresponds with—HER "PAN" PALS

46. **Jumbles:** PROXY HEFTY BALLAD FUNGUS
Answer: What she said when her rejected suitor threatened to jump off the cliff—THAT'S ONLY A "BLUFF"

184

47. **Jumbles:** CYNIC AGING HEARSE SNITCH
Answer: He had no problem keeping up his end of the conversation, but a lot of trouble doing this—REACHING IT

48. **Jumbles:** FAULT BOUGH EFFACE GHETTO
Answer: You'll never lose weight if you try to do no more than this—LAUGH IT OFF

49. **Jumbles:** SMOKY BARGE APATHY MUFFIN
Answer: What the frustrated actor turned butcher knew how to do—HAM IT UP

50. **Jumbles:** KNACK SWOOP LACKEY CROUCH
Answer: What kind of music do you get when you throw a stone into the water?—PLUNK ROCK

51. **Jumbles:** GOING LOBBY DETACH GASKET
Answer: After the Dutch started making wooden shoes, stores were—CLOGGED

52. **Jumbles:** HONEY YIELD GRUMPY WEASEL
Answer: The boy who questioned every request from his parents was a—"WHYS" GUY

53. **Jumbles:** THEFT EVOKE CRANNY WHIMSY
Answer: The child got muddy playing outside and would end up—IN HOT WATER

54. **Jumbles:** SUITE ODDLY HYMNAL LIKELY
Answer: When Burr challenged Hamilton to a battle using pistols, it was—"DUEL-Y" NOTED

55. **Jumbles:** RODEO ELUDE VOLUME THRASH
Answer: Sleepy Hollow's legendary horseman loved his new boots and was—HEAD OVER HEELS

56. **Jumbles:** GIZMO WHISK WINNER OUTAGE
Answer: Before they fully understood flight, the Wright brothers could often be seen—WINGING IT

57. **Jumbles:** ABIDE OUNCE RUDDER SWAMPY
Answer: After asking the Jumble artist to help her get on "The Price Is Right," he—DREW CAREY

58. **Jumbles:** SWEPT WAFER BUSHEL DETECT
Answer: To see where the biggest waves could be ridden, they—SURFED THE WEB

59. **Jumbles:** PLUME TALLY FIGURE ACCORD
Answer: Her old 10-speed was way beyond repair and was at the end of its—LIFE CYCLE

60. **Jumbles:** GIDDY TULIP DECEIT ABSORB
Answer: He blamed another sea lion, but the sea lion said it was the—"OTTER" GUY

61. **Jumbles:** YOUTH BISON BAKERY OUTWIT
Answer: When her brother tied her shoes together, he was being a—"KNOTTY" BOY

62. **Jumbles:** SINGE RUGBY PLEDGE LONGER
Answer: When they found a bag of peanuts at the Grand Canyon, the squirrels—GORGED

63. **Jumbles:** ENVOY SLUSH DIVINE WANTED
Answer: The customer was a pessimist and ordered his eggs—SUNNY-SIDE DOWN

64. **Jumbles:** GUARD CEASE STUDIO SCRIPT
Answer: When the basketball player appeared as a witness, the jury had—COURT-SIDE SEATS

65. **Jumbles:** QUEST HAIRY AGENDA SYRUPY
Answer: The mint where the Washington 25-cent coins were produced was the—HEADQUARTERS

66. **Jumbles:** GAUZE ELECT RADIUS PARLAY
Answer: The book about the moon's effect on the world's oceans had a—"TIDAL" PAGE

67. **Jumbles:** OZONE PUPPY DIGEST RUCKUS
Answer: The chef who was a part-time race car driver drove a car that was—SOUPED UP

68. **Jumbles:** USHER GIANT OUTLAW PASTRY
Answer: Explaining the rules of arm wrestling is simple because it's—EASY TO GRASP

69. **Jumbles:** ABUZZ PERKY SHREWD MALADY
Answer: He announced when Mount Rushmore would be completed to give people a—HEADS UP

70. **Jumbles:** PRIVY RERUN INFANT PHOTON
Answer: Would the weather be clear for their balloon flight? It was—UP IN THE AIR

71. **Jumbles:** DIGIT OUTDO GLANCE FORGOT
Answer: The handyman bought a new truck so he could—TOOL AROUND

72. **Jumbles:** DAISY TAUNT BARBER PUDDLE
Answer: Considered to be exceptionally honest, the judge was—TRIED AND TRUE

73. **Jumbles:** SLANT FRUIT BAMBOO VELVET
Answer: After specializing in miniature sculptures, Willard Wigan made a—SMALL FORTUNE

74. **Jumbles:** PLANT HABIT WILLOW RATIFY
Answer: The marathon's finish wasn't even close. The winner—RAN AWAY WITH IT

75. **Jumbles:** VENUE UNDUE SMOOCH GYRATE
Answer: When asked if he'd bought ample supplies for the party, he said—SURE ENOUGH

76. **Jumbles:** ELDER SHAME PUBLIC OUTAGE
Answer: The archer who scored a bull's-eye to secure her team's victory—AIMED TO PLEASE

77. **Jumbles:** TOXIN FEVER SPOOKY ISLAND
Answer: After bowling a 300 game, people wanted the bowler to—STRIKE A POSE

78. **Jumbles:** ROVER SWIFT UNPACK PADDED
Answer: When the Jumble artist sketched his work area, it included a—DESK DRAWER

79. **Jumbles:** RIGID HARSH LOOSEN SPOTTY
Answer: The baseball team was moving and the jersey seller was about to—LOSE HIS SHIRT

80. **Jumbles:** MAUVE TABOO BANISH PLACID
Answer: When the pirate with the peg leg was told to walk the plank, he was—OUT ON A LIMB

81. **Jumbles:** PROVE WATCH THROWN AFLOAT
Answer: When the alien walked off his spaceship, the people watching said—WHAT ON EARTH?

82. **Jumbles:** SKIMP LEAVE INTENT FORGET
Answer: Everyone watched him pull in the fish—IN "REEL" TIME

83. **Jumbles:** WEIGH DUNCE ENROLL BOUNCE
Answer: It took many workers to man the offshore rig. Together, they drilled for—"CREWED" OIL

84. **Jumbles:** LOGIC WOUND ODDITY FELLOW
Answer: Little Red Riding Hood's "grandmother" was in a hurry to eat and—WOLFED IT DOWN

85. **Jumbles:** CHORD HEDGE MUMBLE BUMMER
Answer: When they replaced all the mattresses at the hotel, it was—MUCH "BEDDER"

86. **Jumbles:** PARTY CHIVE VERSUS FILLET
Answer: At one out away from a perfect game, the crowd's cheering reached a—FEVER PITCH

87. **Jumbles:** THEME CLING CLIQUE GALAXY
Answer: The buffalo nickel was replaced after the mint approved the—EXACT CHANGE

88. **Jumbles:** EXPEL LOOPY REFUSE JOGGER
Answer: Ben Franklin's response to bifocal skeptics was—YOU'LL SEE

89. **Jumbles:** GRIME PILOT JAGGED PIGEON
Answer: He didn't want to pay much for the off-road vehicle and was trying to get it—DIRT "JEEP"

90. **Jumbles:** PANIC TENTH PEBBLE PLURAL
Answer: They built the castle on the highest point so their enemies would have an—UPHILL BATTLE

91. **Jumbles:** SUNNY GLOAT TORRID TOMCAT
Answer: The landscapers at NASA's Johnson Space Center specialized in—GROUND CONTROL

92. **Jumbles:** OZONE HILLY HURRAH MUTTON
Answer: The Swiss cheese at the church picnic had an attitude that was—HOLIER THAN THOU

93. **Jumbles:** PATCH DIZZY GERBIL BUFFET
Answer: Using their high beams at night on the unfamiliar road was a—BRIGHT IDEA

94. **Jumbles:** WHEAT OUNCE FEMALE PERMIT
Answer: The skier gave exact instructions and expected the speedboat driver to—TOW THE LINE

95. **Jumbles:** GRANT PLAID POORLY BRUNCH
Answer: The book about Henry Ford and his car company was an—"AUTO"-BIOGRAPHY

96. **Jumbles:** PRAWN ALIAS BIGGER USEFUL
Answer: When the spies securely placed the hidden listening device, it was—SNUG AS A BUG

97. **Jumbles:** WOUND UTTER MASCOT POETRY
Answer: When the ballet scene featured a duo of ballerinas, all eyes were drawn—TO TWO TUTUS

98. **Jumbles:** DITTO SNIFF POWDER SICKLE
Answer: The ice cream shop employees knew a lot because they had the—INSIDE SCOOP

99. **Jumbles:** WALTZ TABBY IDIOCY AUTHOR
Answer: Her baby was overdue, and the expectant mom was anxious about the—BIRTH "WAIT"

100. **Jumbles:** BLUNT FENCE CANOPY DOLLAR
Answer: Shoddy workmanship at the mirror factory was beginning to—REFLECT BADLY

101. **Jumbles:** SALSA CHAOS FEDORA BURLAP
Answer: The grand opening of the rec center's new pool—CAUSED A SPLASH

102. **Jumbles:** UNWED VIPER GOVERN ORATOR
Answer: The new bartender got to know his customers by establishing a—GOOD "RE-POUR"

103. **Jumbles:** HABIT DEPTH BUTANE WALNUT
Answer: He checked the knots for tightness to see if they'd learned—WHAT HE'D "TAUT"

104. **Jumbles:** FORGO STALL CONCUR HECKLE
Answer: The young detective led the investigation until a senior detective—GOT ON HER CASE

105. **Jumbles:** VILLA AUDIT EXCEED FINALE
Answer: When she wore her new wool Christmas sweater, the Spanish teacher said—"FLEECE" NAVIDAD

106. **Jumbles:** PIXEL MONTH FAMILY DREDGE
Answer: When it came to making presents for her family, the girl was—GIFTED

107. **Jumbles:** NUDGE DWELL AUBURN FAIRLY
Answer: Voting to raise prices more than 500 percent, the selfish business people—ALL "A-GREED"

108. **Jumbles:** VOUCH ENACT MISHAP UNWIND
Answer: The TV anchorman didn't know he was about to be fired. It would soon be—NEWS TO HIM

109. **Jumbles:** VIXEN DIMLY FERVOR GYRATE
Answer: When they installed windmills on the farm, they created an—ENERGY FIELD

110. **Jumbles:** RELIC RAVEN ATTEST DOODLE
Answer: The badly-decaying metal gate at the old mansion was made of—"ROT" IRON

111. **Jumbles:** GUAVA JUICE BUDGET STENCH
Answer: Whether or not gloves or mittens are better was the—SUBJECT AT HAND

112. **Jumbles:** EAGLE MIGHT OUTFIT FINISH
Answer: They'd never put up wallpaper before. It took them a while to—GET THE HANG OF IT

113. **Jumbles:** FANCY ABOUT SHRIMP BURGER
Answer: The televised pool tournament began—RIGHT ON CUE

114. **Jumbles:** FLIRT DECAY URCHIN OPPOSE
Answer: When it became clear they were breaking up, the Beatles were—DONE "FOUR"

115. **Jumbles:** GLAND HENCE GLOBAL MISFIT
Answer: The delays at the skydiving school were a result of—FALLING BEHIND

116. **Jumbles:** GUEST WOMAN KITTEN POLISH
Answer: His attempt to give up cigarettes—WENT UP IN SMOKE

117. **Jumbles:** GEESE GABBY HIDDEN JUNIOR
Answer: The lawyers in the courtroom were—BEING JUDGED

118. **Jumbles:** KOALA KITTY PICNIC FIDDLE
Answer: The theme for the Inspector Clouseau film caused Blake Edwards to be—TICKLED PINK

119. **Jumbles:** HOUSE DRAFT SPRUCE RUNNER
Answer: The court case against the manufacturer of the faulty windows was—OPEN AND SHUT

120. **Jumbles:** AWFUL DRINK BESTOW EXPOSE
Answer: After teaching the scouts how to build a campfire, the troop leader—WAS STOKED

121. **Jumbles:** TWICE METAL GARLIC CRISIS
Answer: The couple who had their sofa re-covered with a very expensive fabric were—MATERIALISTIC

122. **Jumbles:** BLISS GLOAT SPLINT CREAMY
Answer: One day people living in orbit will be able to watch TV on—SPACE STATIONS

123. **Jumbles:** CRAMP OUTDO THEORY FIDDLE
Answer: The lawyers met for lunch at the—FOOD COURT

124. **Jumbles:** DOUSE DERBY SONATA INTENT
Answer: The people waiting to pay for their purchases were—"BUY-STANDERS"

125. **Jumbles:** BIRCH TIGER SHREWD WINDOW
Answer: Their new talking scale had a—"WEIGH" WITH WORDS

126. **Jumbles:** INKED GETUP TRUANT FLINCH
Answer: It was time to get a new lawn mower because the one they had wasn't—CUTTING IT

127. **Jumbles:** MIDST MUNCH INWARD BRONCO
Answer: The remote bed and breakfast allowed the newlyweds to be—"INN-COMMUNICADO"

128. **Jumbles:** BIKER EPOXY FREELY SLEIGH
Answer: Her new glasses were ready and were right—"BE-FOR" HER EYES

129. **Jumbles:** MOUND HUTCH THINLY OPAQUE
Answer: The kangaroo gave her husband a to-do list and expected him to—HOP TO IT

130. **Jumbles:** TULIP BYLAW CIRCUS NODDED
Answer: The process for making beef jerky is—CUT-AND-DRY

131. **Jumbles:** SNOWY GECKO SPRAIN CHORUS
Answer: When the lions figured out how to build a fire, it was a—ROARING SUCCESS

132. **Jumbles:** SWOON DIVOT THIRTY ACCUSE
Answer: When the stand-up comedian ran out of new ideas, he was—AT HIS WIT'S END

133. **Jumbles:** TRAWL COUPE STEREO SLUSHY
Answer: The boutique was going out of business, so they had a—"CLOTHES-OUT" SALE

134. **Jumbles:** MODEM HIKER RATIFY REJECT
Answer: William Clement invented the grandfather clock because he was able to—MAKE THE TIME

135. **Jumbles:** HAIRY LATCH WALLET COFFEE
Answer: The spare didn't always fit in with the other four tires and often felt like a—FIFTH WHEEL

136. **Jumbles:** WAGER WINCE NATIVE PELLET
Answer: The stage performers often had problems—INTERACTING

137. **Jumbles:** GOOEY HARSH WETTER NAPKIN
Answer: The guitarist came up with a new melody, but didn't think it was—WORTH NOTING

138. **Jumbles:** DINKY PRONG SICKEN VIABLE
Answer: The carp that hid behind the rock in the garden pool was—BEING "KOI"

139. **Jumbles:** OMEGA WIPER CONNED TIDIER
Answer: They wanted to go bowling. They just needed to—
PIN DOWN A TIME

140. **Jumbles:** FAVOR TRUNK MISUSE WEALTH
Answer: The deer gave birth and knew what to do thanks to her—MOTHER NATURE

141. **Jumbles:** BUSHY GROUP TRUSTY HIGHER
Answer: For America to become a pioneer in the aviation industry, it took the—"RIGHT" BROTHERS

142. **Jumbles:** FACET SHIFT GLOOMY ORIGIN
Answer: The subdivision where they chose to build their dream home had—LOTS TO OFFER

143. **Jumbles:** TWEAK BURST GROUND FEISTY
Answer: After receiving a patent for the rubber heel, Humphrey O'Sullivan made—GREAT STRIDES

144. **Jumbles:** SWAMP YOUNG INDUCT CAMERA
Answer: The new human-powered Greek ship would be able to stay at sea for—DAYS IN A ROW

145. **Jumbles:** FINCH EMPTY WILLOW COPPER
Answer: He needed to get started on his new novel and would begin—"WRITE" NOW

146. **Jumbles:** OOMPH YIELD VALLEY VIEWED
Answer: The pigeons had been married for years but were still—LOVEY-DOVEY

147. **Jumbles:** SHIFT PHOTO CACTUS EYEFUL
Answer: When the anchorman was told there was a pursuit in progress, he—CUT TO THE CHASE

148. **Jumbles:** SEIZE BRAND SCORCH PLAQUE
Answer: The flight attendants were under a lot of stress and were feeling the—CABIN PRESSURE

149. **Jumbles:** GROVE BERTH SPIRAL INWARD
Answer: When they played cards in view of the Golden Gate, they were—BRIDGE PARTNERS

150. **Jumbles:** VISOR TRACT WIGGLE FEWEST
Answer: Many people saw "Star Wars" multiple times and gave it—GREAT "RE-VIEWS"

151. **Jumbles:** ABATE MESSY ACCENT SKIMPY
Answer: She could hand-sew a hem very quickly and made it—"SEAM" EASY

152. **Jumbles:** KNELT BROOM SCENIC HAIRDO
Answer: The Toll House Inn's Ruth Wakefield, the creator of chocolate chips, was—ONE SMART COOKIE

153. **Jumbles:** PUTTY WHEEL ENTICE TOFFEE
Answer: The horse wanted to take dancing lessons but was worried about his—TWO LEFT FEET

154. **Jumbles:** IRONY PIANO GLADLY TUMBLE
Answer: When the track coach's stopwatch wouldn't work, it was—BAD TIMING

155. **Jumbles:** ANNUL ENSUE GRITTY DEVOUR
Answer: When their brand-new heating/cooling system broke again, he—VENTED HIS ANGER

156. **Jumbles:** HOUND BRIBE INDIGO GROGGY
Answer: The ant's eggs hatched, and she didn't mind a bit when the babies started—BUGGING HER

157. **Jumbles:** DIRTY SKIMP EXTENT HECTIC
Answer: Her husband smelled horrible after his sweaty workout, so she gave him the—STINK EYE

158. **Jumbles:** FEVER OBESE SAILOR MOMENT
Answer: Between the Baltic and the Mediterranean, they visited sites—FROM "SEE" TO "SEE"

159. **Jumbles:** SKULL ABIDE JOGGER NESTLE
Answer: When "The Untouchables" began airing in 1959, viewers tuned in—LIKE GANGBUSTERS

160. **Jumbles:** THICK OUTDO UNEASY TIPTOE
Answer: Her grandparents gave her their old car, and she really—TOOK A SHINE TO IT

161. **Jumbles:** CAMPUS FAMISH LIQUOR PICKET INTAKE DIVERT
Answer: He hoped to make lots of money in textiles because he was inclined to be this—"MATERIALISTIC"

162. **Jumbles:** POMADE HUNGRY GARISH ADJOIN NIBBLE CHOSEN
Answer: What they called the gangster who moved next door—THE "NEIGHBOR HOOD"

163. **Jumbles:** EMPLOY SCENIC BANANA GUTTER CLEAVE DEMISE
Answer: The first duty of the missionary was to convert the cannibals to this—VEGETARIANISM

164. **Jumbles:** CLUMSY TRIBAL ACCENT BOLERO SURELY QUARTZ
Answer: The kind of people you might meet at the information bureau—"QUESTIONABLE" ONES

165. **Jumbles:** JERSEY CUPFUL PALLID VENDOR ABLAZE BEMOAN
Answer: What that love letter was calculated to do—SPEED UP THE "MALE"

166. **Jumbles:** SHOULD GENIUS INVITE MOSTLY NOBODY SCULPT
Answer: The abacus seller's business had prospered which allowed him to—COUNT HIS BLESSINGS

167. **Jumbles:** THATCH TARIFF GAMBIT SURELY BARREN COBALT
Answer: The meal at the fancy restaurant was delicious, but they were having problems—STOMACHING THE BILL

168. **Jumbles:** HARDLY SHADOW GRILLE GROCER PRANCE UPROOT
Answer: The thief who stole credit card numbers and used them to make purchases was—GUILTY AS CHARGED

169. **Jumbles:** FOURTH ENCORE WRITER EXPAND AURORA VOLUME
Answer: When Canada replaced its flag in 1965 with its current flag, they—TURNED OVER A NEW LEAF

170. **Jumbles:** STIGMA GARISH MULLET GOSSIP FUTURE WORTHY
Answer: The computer coder wanted his lazy co-worker to—GET WITH THE PROGRAM

171. **Jumbles:** COSMOS GENTLE TRUDGE CANCAN WIDGET SWIVEL
Answer: California's famous "muscle beach" outdoor gym started in 1934 and is—STILL GOING STRONG

172. **Jumbles:** PLACID GOATEE ABSURD DEVICE NOTIFY SPLASH
Answer: The quarterback's performance was improving with—EACH PASSING DAY

173. **Jumbles:** IMPACT FLAUNT ORNERY DETACH WOODSY WEASEL
Answer: The store only sold gloves, mittens and shoes, and customers were—WAITED ON HAND AND FOOT

174. **Jumbles:** CURFEW CACKLE GOTTEN BROKER SMOOCH WALLOW
Answer: The fashion model refused to try on anything and would soon—WEAR OUT HER WELCOME

175. **Jumbles:** CLOSET GLANCE SUPERB EITHER IRONIC THROWN
Answer: Her jeans had worn out and were—
ON THEIR LAST LEGS

176. **Jumbles:** WEASEL CRUNCH MENACE FLAUNT EYELID CLASSY
Answer: The distance between NYC and L.A. in a passenger jet is 2,500 miles—AS THE "CREW" FLIES

177. **Jumbles:** FROSTY CASHEW EQUITY ADVENT DEGREE HICCUP
Answer: The successful launch of the first instant lottery tickets just—SCRATCHED THE SURFACE

178. **Jumbles:** QUIVER NEARLY RADIAL PEANUT AFRAID THEORY
Answer: The St. Patrick's Day festivities were ready to begin, but they hoped it wouldn't—RAIN ON THEIR PARADE

179. **Jumbles:** BOUNTY UNSURE VISUAL MODEST IMPALA SHRIMP
Answer: After Evel Knievel's early success performing motorcycle jumps, he was able to—RAMP UP HIS BUSINESS

180. **Jumbles:** IMPACT SHABBY FLORAL FENNEL FIASCO TIGHTS
Answer: Boeing became a huge airplane manufacturer after getting—OFF TO A FLYING START

Need More Jumbles®?

Jumble® Books

More than 175 puzzles each!

Cowboy Jumble®
$10.95 • ISBN: 978-1-62937-355-3

Jammin' Jumble®
$9.95 • ISBN: 978-1-57243-844-6

Java Jumble®
$10.95 • ISBN: 978-1-60078-415-6

Jet Set Jumble®
$9.95 • ISBN: 978-1-60078-353-1

Jolly Jumble®
$10.95 • ISBN: 978-1-60078-214-5

Jumble® Anniversary
$10.95 • ISBN: 987-1-62937-734-6

Jumble® Ballet
$10.95 • ISBN: 978-1-62937-616-5

Jumble® Birthday
$10.95 • ISBN: 978-1-62937-652-3

Jumble® Celebration
$10.95 • ISBN: 978-1-60078-134-6

Jumble® Champion
$10.95 • ISBN: 978-1-62937-870-1

Jumble® Christmas
$10.95 • ISBN: 978-1-63727-182-7

Jumble® Coronation
$10.95 • ISBN: 978-1-62937-976-0

Jumble® Cuisine
$10.95 • ISBN: 978-1-62937-735-3

Jumble® Drag Race
$9.95 • ISBN: 978-1-62937-483-3

Jumble® Ever After
$10.95 • ISBN: 978-1-62937-785-8

Jumble® Explorer
$9.95 • ISBN: 978-1-60078-854-3

Jumble® Explosion
$10.95 • ISBN: 978-1-60078-078-3

Jumble® Fever
$9.95 • ISBN: 978-1-57243-593-3

Jumble® Galaxy
$10.95 • ISBN: 978-1-60078-583-2

Jumble® Garden
$10.95 • ISBN: 978-1-62937-653-0

Jumble® Genius
$10.95 • ISBN: 978-1-57243-896-5

Jumble® Geography
$10.95 • ISBN: 978-1-62937-615-8

Jumble® Getaway
$10.95 • ISBN: 978-1-60078-547-4

Jumble® Gold
$10.95 • ISBN: 978-1-62937-354-6

Jumble® Jackpot
$10.95 • ISBN: 978-1-57243-897-2

Jumble® Jailbreak
$9.95 • ISBN: 978-1-62937-002-6

Jumble® Jambalaya
$9.95 • ISBN: 978-1-60078-294-7

Jumble® Jitterbug
$10.95 • ISBN: 978-1-60078-584-9

Jumble® Journey
$10.95 • ISBN: 978-1-62937-549-6

Jumble® Jubilation
$10.95 • ISBN: 978-1-62937-784-1

Jumble® Jubilee
$10.95 • ISBN: 978-1-57243-231-4

Jumble® Juggernaut
$9.95 • ISBN: 978-1-60078-026-4

Jumble® Kingdom
$10.95 • ISBN: 978-1-62937-079-8

Jumble® Knockout
$9.95 • ISBN: 978-1-62937-078-1

Jumble® Madness
$10.95 • ISBN: 978-1-892049-24-7

Jumble® Magic
$9.95 • ISBN: 978-1-60078-795-9

Jumble® Mania
$10.95 • ISBN: 978-1-57243-697-8

Jumble® Marathon
$9.95 • ISBN: 978-1-60078-944-1

Jumble® Masterpiece
$10.95 • ISBN: 978-1-62937-916-6

Jumble® Neighbor
$10.95 • ISBN: 978-1-62937-845-9

Jumble® Parachute
$10.95 • ISBN: 978-1-62937-548-9

Jumble® Party
$10.95 • ISBN: 978-1-63727-008-0

Jumble® Safari
$9.95 • ISBN: 978-1-60078-675-4

Jumble® Sensation
$10.95 • ISBN: 978-1-60078-548-1

Jumble® Skyscraper
$10.95 • ISBN: 978-1-62937-869-5

Jumble® Symphony
$10.95 • ISBN: 978-1-62937-131-3

Jumble® Theater
$9.95 • ISBN: 978-1-62937-484-0

Jumble® Time Machine: 1972
$10.95 • ISBN: 978-1-63727-082-0

Jumble® Trouble
$10.95 • ISBN: 978-1-62937-917-3

Jumble® University
$10.95 • ISBN: 978-1-62937-001-9

Jumble® Unleashed
$10.95 • ISBN: 978-1-62937-844-2

Jumble® Vacation
$10.95 • ISBN: 978-1-60078-796-6

Jumble® Wedding
$9.95 • ISBN: 978-1-62937-307-2

Jumble® Workout
$10.95 • ISBN: 978-1-60078-943-4

Jump, Jive and Jumble®
$9.95 • ISBN: 978-1-60078-215-2

Lunar Jumble®
$9.95 • ISBN: 978-1-60078-853-6

Monster Jumble®
$10.95 • ISBN: 978-1-62937-213-6

Mystic Jumble®
$9.95 • ISBN: 978-1-62937-130-6

Rainy Day Jumble®
$10.95 • ISBN: 978-1-60078-352-4

Royal Jumble®
$10.95 • ISBN: 978-1-60078-738-6

Sports Jumble®
$10.95 • ISBN: 978-1-57243-113-3

Summer Fun Jumble®
$10.95 • ISBN: 978-1-57243-114-0

Touchdown Jumble®
$9.95 • ISBN: 978-1-62937-212-9

Oversize Jumble® Books

More than 500 puzzles!

Colossal Jumble®
$19.95 • ISBN: 978-1-57243-490-5

Jumbo Jumble®
$19.95 • ISBN: 978-1-57243-314-4

Jumble® Crosswords™

More than 175 puzzles!

Jumble® Crosswords™
$10.95 • ISBN: 978-1-57243-347-2